Grief of a Parent and Loss

Navigating and Coping With Grief After the Death of a Parent

Cortez Ranieri

Table of Contents

Introduction

Grief is an instinctive reaction to loss. Whenever a beloved materialistic or non-materialistic item is taken away, you experience an emotional turmoil called grief.

In our lifetime, we experience gain and loss. It's important to learn ways to deal with loss and the emotions that come with it. Grief is a healthy way of processing the changes in your life. Shock, anger, betrayal, and sadness are all a part of the process. Initially, you're overwhelmed by all the thoughts and emotions—especially when you lose something or someone that you love.

Grief can cause mental and emotional instability, but if you don't start handling it well, it can disrupt your physical health as well. Your physical health comes to an extreme. You're either binge eating or barely eating. You're either oversleeping or find it difficult to sleep at all. You feel lost. You have frequent thoughts about that person. Good memories, fights, arguments, love, or regrets. There's no between. It's the way your body reacts and copes with the way you feel.

The intensity of your grief is determined by how significant your loss was to you and whether it was expected or not. Each tragedy and person is different. For example, losing a parent can cause you months or years of profound sadness, but losing a bicycle might make you sad just for a few days. Grief can be caused due to various reasons like the death of a loved one, financial losses, separation from your partner, illness, or family problems.

There are rituals performed to express grief as a society. It's usually a funeral or a silent gathering to honor the person's life. It allows close ones to come together in support of one another. Being with people who share your grief can help you feel better. You know you're not alone in it. Close relatives come to visit you, spend time, and share different memories. This is just the beginning of the next couple of days where people visit you to give their condolences. When these rituals end, everyone assumes that you should be done grieving and move on with your life. But you don't need to cave in these expectations.

Rituals, however, are just the start of your grieving process. You might also find it difficult to concentrate on your daily activities. This is another part of grief—smiling on the outside to show other people you've moved on, but you're still processing it all. A personal loss is nothing to be ashamed about. You deserve to grieve and process your loss. When someone you love has died, it's natural for you to be shaken up. You start having feelings and questions about everything. You don't know what the next step is, or how to deal with a situation like this. You gradually start to feel better. With time, you will start to heal. This book will help you find ways to process your emotions so, as time passes, you get better and stronger. You embark upon this journey of healing to come out as a stronger and more resilient person.

Personally, my biggest moment of grief occurred when I was just 14 years old. I lost my mother to cancer. This was the most difficult loss I've ever had to face. I encountered various challenges at a young age, which no kid deserves to go through. But through building the right habits and getting the help that I needed, I've managed to overcome those hardships. It felt like a loss of love, care, affection, and nurture. Since then, I've wanted to understand loss and grief in a deeper sense. To research it extensively.

The reason I wanted to write this book is to help people on a similar journey. I was fortunate enough to get the right help, but many people may be lost and broken by their grief. After experiencing the loss of a parent first-hand, I knew I wanted to help people get through their loss and mental hurdles. Feeling dissociated from society and myself was my biggest challenge. The world is constantly moving, and you're expected to move on quickly. Especially in the world of social media, where you see people constantly move on to the next thing, you feel stuck and distracted. The way you decide to cope is completely up to you. Don't let social media or society decide the way you behave or react to situations. This book is going to provide you with guidance and a framework that you can personally mold and apply to your situation.

Losing a mother made me feel handicapped. As a child, you're hardwired to look at them for love, support, and guidance. On the other hand, the loss of a father can compromise your future vision, knowledge, guidance, purpose, and commitment. Losing a mother, though, is often more grueling because of the closeness and bond. That said, it also depends on your unique relationship with each of them. They are an invisible force who pushes you to achieve your dreams and now they are no longer with you. This can be a traumatic experience irrespective of your age. A lot of people don't understand grief and the ways to deal with it.

This book will guide you to cope with such losses in a healthy manner. You will find ways to support yourself during this difficult phase. It's not only to cope with grief, but also to come to terms with their absence. To let them go peacefully as we forgive them. This doesn't mean you forget about their existence, however. They'll always be a part of you. Yet, you'll start becoming responsible for your own life instead of being sheltered by your parents. It's a growth you can choose to embrace.

It might be difficult in the beginning stages, but you don't have to do it all at once. Taking baby steps and slowly starting to develop habits and attitudes can help you regain control over your life. Losing a parent can be an eye-opening opportunity to change our lives, but it's the way you decide to take this news that will determine your path ahead. After all, our families are the first relationship we have. It's the longest, most permanent, and impactful relationship of our life. It's rare to completely break a family bond. So, grieving for the loss of a family member can be a personal process as it depends on multiple elements, including your faith, personality, the significance of your loss, and your coping style.

Most people believe that ignoring your pain will make it go away quicker. Unfortunately, trying to avoid or suppress the pain will leave emotional scars in the long run. You need to actively feel your emotions. You can't heal the emotions that you don't feel. If you keep suppressing your emotions, you'll develop wounds you're unaware of. The kind of wound that will bleed on others. You don't need to act or pretend to be strong. Modern society tells you to "Move on," "Find closure," "Be strong," or "Get over it." Don't give your pain any more power than it already has. Don't end your relationship with someone because of death. Your love for something that you've lost is immortal. So, don't let mortality take away the power of your love.

Love for another person doesn't die, even if they do. Feeling sad or frightened is a normal response. Crying at the loss of a close loved one doesn't make you "weak," it makes you a human. Don't let gender stereotypes define the way you mourn for your loss. Crying doesn't make you weak, and not crying doesn't mean you're not sorry for your loss. Let your feelings naturally surface without any judgments. You're allowed to cry, but don't start crying because "you're a man and you shouldn't be crying." You're angry at your mother's death, but now you're angry for being angry. Judging your negative feelings will only give them more power.

Go through the process, however ugly it looks. You will move on when the time is right for you. The aim to process our grief is to remember our deceased ones with more love and affection.

Chapter 1:

The Reason Losing Your

Parents Is so Hurtful

As kids, we look to our parents for everything. We believe that they are superheroes— invincible forces that cannot be defeated at any cost. Their presence in your life is unwavering. Losing a parent as a kid or as an adult can be equally difficult. You could be three or 30 years old, yet the intensity of the impact doesn't change. Even as adults, we are hardwired to depend on our parents for certain emotional and materialistic needs. We are aware that the death of our parents is inevitable, yet it's one of the most painful experiences a human has to suffer through. You expect your parents to attend and support every milestone of your life—graduation, marriage, kids, and eventually retirement. The absence of their support at each milestone can leave an extreme feeling of emptiness within you. Their support and guidance are critical.

There's an unspoken expectation that, as an adult, it's easier to move on from a child's death than a parents'. You're aware that your parents will cease to exist one day, of course, but that doesn't prepare you for the grief that you're going to face. You're expected to accept death easier and faster. To handle your loss responsibly and in an adult manner. You're not allowed to lose your calm and composure. You cannot be seen crying and/or losing your cool. You aren't allowed to express your sadness.

These societal expectations will only burden you and be more damaging in the long run. You're not expected to deal with grief by yourself—and shouldn't. That's underestimating grief. That's diminishing pain in an unhealthy way and putting pressure on someone based on age or maturity. Yes, it may not affect your teen years, which are crucial for your growth, but that doesn't lessen the emotional and mental damage.

People often comment during the funeral, "You should be grateful your father lived a long and complete life" or "It's good your mother died quick, without any pain or suffering." These sentences don't resonate with the loss of a parent. The misconception that an adult wouldn't grieve for a long time leaves the person feeling lonelier than before. Should you be grateful that your parents lived a happy life? Yes. But does that have to be the first response to your loss? No.

It's okay to take as much time as you need. People start to get impatient with your grieving, so be mindful of who you trust with your innermost feelings. Most people experience a variety of negative emotions including hurt, sadness, and betrayal. There are different stages of experiencing these emotions which we will be discussing in the next chapter.

As your parent's child, you either had a rocky relationship full of ups and downs, or you had a close connection where you confided in them all the time. So, when your mother or father passes away, it's natural to start reflecting on their journey and your contribution to their life. In fact, you may find yourself asking questions like: *How was my relationship with my parents? What were the challenges? How did my relationship with them make me feel? Do I have any regrets? If so, what are those? If I could go back in time, what are the things I would change?*

Additionally, you may start evaluating your decisions and actions. You may question the words you spoke and the way you treated them: *Was I too hard on them? Did I actually mean the things I said?* In grief, it's not uncommon for your viewpoint on the relationship to change.

Our relationship with our parents evolves with time. Whether you walk alone on your journey ahead or with a single parent, your perspective of them and the world around you shifts—even the smallest of things and thoughts. Previously, you had your parents to shield you from anything that happens. But now you're no longer in this shield created by your parents. You need to face the world and your life as it comes. That's all grief at work. This is why you cannot expect yourself to jump back into your daily routine as if nothing happened. You have to adjust to a new sense of normal. A new way of living. You'll have to start filling in the role your parents left vacant. For instance, taking care of yourself when you're sick if your mother passes away, or learning how to do your own taxes if you've lost your father.

You may find emptiness in many moments after your parents pass away but moving on doesn't mean you forget about their existence. It means making peace with their absence and knowing that they love you. That they are proud of you in the moments you truly need them.

Grief in itself is very complicated. It can open you up to a myriad of difficult emotions you may have never felt before. So, when you're experiencing grief for the first time, the intensity may feel overwhelming. This is especially true if your parents' passing was sudden or unexpected.

In best-case scenarios, the loss of a parent can be anticipated. Perhaps they had a known or chronic illness that slowly deteriorated their health over time. Perhaps their healthcare provider had told you a proposed time limit that your parents had left. Perhaps you'd had discussions with your parents in their last days and had had the opportunity to prepare yourself mentally and emotionally. In cases like these, you're given the chance to say goodbye and have closure.

However, this doesn't always happen. Sometimes death happens out of the blue. Your parents seem at the peak of health one day and are gone the next. Or, worse, one or both of your parents passes away suddenly due to a heart attack or an accident. Unexpected or sudden death like this does not allow time to say goodbye or get closure and can lead to a longer period of time where you struggle with denial and/or anger.

As we've previously discussed, the circumstances under which your parents pass away can have a big impact on your grieving process. For instance, a sudden death is harder to wrap our minds around than as compared to an anticipated death and can cause unresolved grief. Unresolved grief, in turn, can also cause emotional instability like anxiety, depression, or even PTSD. In the short term, it can cause a lot of distress. But if not dealt with in the right way, it can cause permanent issues such as immune disorders, hypertension, and cardiac disorders. This can eventually become a part of your genetics which will then be passed onto future generations. Lastly, when a parent commits suicide, it has the worst impact on the child. The child is filled with guilt, remorse, and feelings of abandonment.

Despite all the self-help books available on grief, there is no one way to grieve. Grief affects everyone differently, which adds to the challenge and uncertainty of how to handle it. How to cope and learn to move on healthfully. This is an important thing to note as you are going through your own grieving process—it's an individual journey.

Depending on the circumstances in which your parent died, you may experience shock before grief. Or you may be able to temporarily ignore your grief altogether. You may be able to plan the memorial and graveside services and smoothly wrap up your parents' estate. You may even be able to go about your job and day-today life for a little while at first. There are many people who are able to do this, so that they are free to grieve afterwards.

On the other hand, you may face grief head-on. You may find it suddenly challenging to carry on with regular life. Where simply getting out of bed every day is too much. Where you cannot fathom the reality of your parents' death, and all you want to do is wake up from the nightmare and get back to the life you've always known. The life where they were alive and well. If this is your experience with grief, you may need to take a complete break from everything, and live life as if you don't exist for a little while.

Surprisingly, the gender of both the parent and child can especially influence the contours of the grief response to a loss. Studies suggest that daughters have more intense grief responses to the loss of their parents than sons. This isn't to say men aren't significantly affected by a parent's death, but they may take a longer time to process their feelings, and ultimately be slower to move on. "Males tend to show emotions less and compartmentalize more," says Carla Marie Manly, a clinical psychologist, and author. "These factors do affect the ability to accept and process grief." (Krisch, 2019). Although sadness is normal, it's okay to not feel it or have something else going on. You might feel numb or okay with their death, as they no longer have to suffer or be in pain. Your feelings are valid, even if they don't fit into the textbook terms of grief. It's a difficult process, but one that's worth going through.

If you don't allow yourself to process these emotions, it will start affecting the way you feel and behave in your other relationships. Not just a romantic one, but the way you feel towards your family and friends might shift. So, share the beautiful memories that you created with your parents. Talk to your family members about what a loving and joyous mother or father you had. Tell your children about their grandmother or grandfather. Keep her alive in your memories and heart through conversations. It might be painful to reminisce her memories initially, but with time, it will only bring a smile to your face. The pain will slowly start to fade as you realize that remembering her is one of the ways to keep her next to you as you move forward with life. No matter what scenario you fall into, it's okay. Either way is completely natural. Struggling to maintain your normal life Distancing yourself from friends and family. Taking bereavement leave from work. All of this is part of grieving.

However, this doesn't mean that you can shut down completely. Finding a balance is the key to healthy grieving. It's good to have distractions here and there, but not to the point where you avoid confronting your emotions. Make room for your feelings as you navigate your life forward. Self-care might be the last thing on your mind, but it's an important aspect to recovering from your loss.

My mom died when I was 14. Many times, I'd wake up and think to myself: *Did all this happen?* It took me a very long time (probably a few years) to find the right balance between experiencing my emotions and distracting myself. In such situations, balance is the key to healthy grieving. You cannot abandon everything, nor should you take up more work than you normally would. It's good to have a distraction but not to the point where you avoid confronting your emotions. Make room for your feelings as you navigate your life forward. Self-care might be the last thing on your mind, but it's an important aspect of recovering from your loss.

Treat yourself with the same kindness you do with your friends and family. Don't think that you have to feel a certain way. Let your emotions flow. You're the only person who can provide comfort 24 hours a day. Self-compassion should be your priority. It has healing powers that can help you and the people around you. It makes you a nicer person in difficult times.

If you are the type of person who constantly goes out of your way to provide love, comfort, and support to a friend who's facing a personal loss, it's time you do the same for yourself. Get as much sleep as you can. Staying up late at night to overthink your past or future will not benefit you in your present. Making up different scenarios in your head to rectify what's already done will not change anything or bring your parents back. Instead, try meditation or exercising. Put together a sleepy time playlist or have some warm tea to help put yourself to sleep. Avoid any caffeine at least three to four hours before bed. Stray away from any kind of substance or alcohol consumption. You might think it'll make the pain vanish for a while, but it's only going to deteriorate your physical and mental health. The numbing sensation it'll provide you is only temporary. What's more, alcohol can make it difficult to process your emotions.

Keep your bedroom dark and cool and snuggle into your blankets. Avoid any social media or TV before bed, so no negative news disturbs your sleep. If you're oversleeping for a little while, know that it's okay to do it. You might need more rest than usual as grieving can soak up a lot of your energy.

If sleep is more elusive, keep a diary next to your bed to record any thoughts lingering in your mind or three things that you're thankful for. Brain dumping is a healthy way to help your mind relax. Likewise, writing down what you're thankful for helps your thoughts stay positive. It's a technique called practicing gratitude, and helps you remind yourself that there's a good side to life as well.

Even during the worst situations, you will find goodness in the smallest of things. It's all about your perspective. Writing down things that you're grateful for will shift your mindset from a bad situation to a good one. Doing this repeatedly will reprogram your mind to find the silver lining in every situation.

While you're grieving, your appetite may take a strong hit, where you're either barely eating or overeating. However, it's important to still eat healthy and try to have three meals a day. Fulfilling your appetite and drinking enough water will give your body the strength you require. It'll also give you that extra energy your body needs. Take deep breaths. Breathing mindfully will bring your attention to the present moment and help you release anxiety. Focus on the way your breathing makes you feel. You'll soon start releasing anxiety and it'll be replaced with calmness. Even gentle exercises like yoga or running can help you feel calm. It takes your attention off the flight or fight response that overthinking can cause.

In the case of immense grief, you can practice this simple method anywhere, multiple times a day. Meditation can be an enormous help. Whether this is through reciting mantras, prayers, mindfulness, breathing exercises, or guided visualization, there are many beneficial meditations that can help you cope. Instead of flowing with your thoughts and emotions, you take control of them. You decide the way you want to feel.

We are so used to being carried away with the way we think or feel that the never-ending negative thoughts don't stop. You live in the same loop. Meditation can help you break your loop of negativity and give you the chance to actively practice the way you want to feel. Regularly practicing meditation will help you shift your emotions to more joyful and happier thoughts.

The length of your meditation is not as essential as its frequency. The more often you practice, the more your body becomes in tune with the way you want to feel. You can start with just two minutes a day, and then work your way up to 20 minutes or more. Taking a walk in nature, going for a hike, or just surrounding yourself with nature can help you ground and reconnect with yourself.

Remember to be realistic about the things you expect from yourself. You're aware that you're not in the space to work at your full capacity, and that's okay. You don't need to feel pressured by the workaround you. Know your boundaries and do only what you can. Even if it's just waking up to drink coffee, that's okay for now. Don't try to push yourself out of your comfort zone as it can worsen your mental and physical health.

In times like these, it's okay to be a little selfish and prioritize your needs. Say no to something you don't feel up to, so that you can say yes to yourself. Learn to handle and manage yourself before helping someone else. Instead of making to-do lists, make a list of things you have already accomplished. You're aware that you're not in your best zone. So, avoid putting pressure on yourself to complete a certain number of tasks. Instead, celebrate small victories. It doesn't have to be anything big or work-related. It can be something as simple as brushing your teeth in the morning. Whatever it is, giving yourself permission to be okay with baby steps and accomplishing little things will give you a sense of achievement and motivate you to move ahead.

Practice something that you're good at and makes you happy. Immerse your skills and abilities into something that you're truly passionate about. It could be dancing, writing, painting, traveling, gardening—or even something as simple as going for a walk with your headphones on or walking your dog. It's a distraction that will help you get in the flow and live in the present moment. It will help you get out of your mind and focus on something that you already love.

Creativity can be another good outlet for your emotions. Adult coloring books, knitting, journaling, drawing—all of these activities, as well as others, can make you more resilient and increase your sense of well-being. They can also help you manage your stress and allow you to express your grief in ways other things cannot.

If you find that releasing your grief through art helps you, consider writing or drawing your emotions to your parents. Let them know that you're sad, angry, or confused. If you're in shock, disbelief, or denial. Doing this can serve as a good emotional outlet, make you feel lighter and give you mental clarity and closure about your parents' death.

It might be difficult to talk to your family about missing your parents or loved ones, but don't be afraid to open up or be vulnerable with them. Remember that they are grieving too.

If there's ever a time in your grief where your emotions are all over the place, and you need extra help sorting everything out, remember that you can always seek professional help. A counselor or therapist will not only listen to you, but also help you healthily navigate your emotions. Especially if you didn't have a positive relationship with your parents, a mental health professional can guide you on the right path. For, the sad truth is that not everyone has positive or happy memories of their parents. Some have traumatic childhoods, abusive parents, or just felt unloved or unaccepted at home. If there was never resolution or a conversation to help address these issues, it can make it more difficult to heal and move on from their death.

This book talks about a lot of similar ideas and concepts that can help you figure out your path through grief. It's not going to help you magically heal your wounds, but it will guide and support you as you seek to heal your emotional wounds. Healing is not linear growth. It has ups and downs to traverse before you find your true north and stabilize yourself.

Yet, I can guarantee that reading the following chapters will be worth it, and help you overcome your grief. That you'll gain insight into healthy grieving strategies and have the support you need. You'll come out on the other side a stronger and better human.

Chapter 2:

Grief Is Real

Any negative change can cause grief. It can either be the death of a loved one, getting fired from a job, being unemployed or a breakup. If you don't process your grief the right way, it can be triggered in your future in multiple instances. For example, the death anniversary of your loved one or when you see your ex-partner with a new romantic interest. The grief will return only when it's suppressed instead of healed.

At some point in time, everyone will experience grief at least once, and there are certain stages of grief that you may go through. There's no particular timeline for any of these phases, however. Each person takes their own time, depending on how deeply the person is affected. None of these stages are unusual. Everyone grieves in their own way. But there are some commonalities in everyone's journey, and the order in which their journey progresses. When you progress through each of these phases, it's a step ahead in your healing journey.

Many researchers have dedicated years of their studies to understand grief and loss better. One of them was a Swiss-American psychiatrist named Elizabeth Kübler-Ross who first introduced her five-stage grief model in her book, *On Death and Dying*. Kübler-Ross' model was based on her work with terminally ill patients and has received much criticism in the years since, mainly because people studying her model mistakenly believed it was the specific order that people were meant to grieve, and that everyone goes through all the stages. Kübler-Ross now notes that these stages are not linear. That some people may experience all of them, and others may not experience any of them. Still others might only undergo two stages rather than all five, one stage, three stages, etc. It is now more readily known that these five stages of grief are the most commonly observed experienced by the grieving population. (Gregory, 2016)

Kübler-Ross received a lot of hate when these five stages did not align. That's when these five stages were adapted and co-written by David Kessler in their book, *On Grief and Grieving,* where it's mentioned that the journey is not linear—you can skip or repeat stages, and there's no timeline for it. You can feel one stage right now, jump to another one and then be back on the first one. The stages can last for minutes or hours while jumping back and forth. Your grief is as unique as your DNA. These five stages are more generalized, basic stages that have been observed in most cases.

Now, let's understand the six stages of grief.

Denial

Grief is an overwhelming feeling that we are not quite ready to handle. The news is too big for us to handle or believe. Your body and mind will accept only the news that it can take without completely collapsing. We cannot fathom the loss that we have to go through. That's why we try to deny the existence of the event. We pretend as if the occurrence never happened. This stage helps us to survive a recent loss. We are yet in shock of what happened and, since we cannot digest the event that has occurred, we deny its existence. This phase helps us to gradually take in the news instead of doing it all at once.

It's essential to try and live one day at a time. Denying helps our feelings to slow down. We pace ourselves to slowly feel and accept instead of feeling every emotion at once. We allow ourselves to think and feel only what we can handle and accept. This has unknowingly started the healing process. This is a common defense mechanism that helps you numb the intense pain. You start realizing that life after this will never be the same. You cannot accept the change, so you start blaming other people or situations for it. You doubt the reality because you don't want that to be true. For example, if you've just been diagnosed with a terminal disease, you won't be able to accept it. You'll blame the nurses for exchanging the reports, or the doctors for mixing up your blood. If the news is the death of a loved one, then you'll blame the doctors for not trying hard enough or that the body has not been recognized correctly. If you're going through a breakup, you hope that your partner will come back to you and that you'll be together again.

You're living in the preferable reality, instead of the actual reality. You have these made-up scenarios in your mind. The preferable reality helps you stagger the impact of the event. The numbness helps you explore your emotions at your speed. Once the denial phases out, you slowly start realizing your reality, and the emotions that were suppressed will come to the surface. All the sorrow that you've denied will rise and you start asking yourself questions such as, how could this happen to me? You feel as if nothing else matters anymore. Especially when a loved one dies, you think you'll never be able to move on from this. Life has changed within minutes. You would have spoken to them last night or just last week and now to never speak to them again is impossible. You feel lost and clueless. Your healing journey continues as you start feeling and questioning everything around you.

Anger

Pain can take various forms, and one of the most common forms is anger. Once you start living in the actual reality instead of preferred reality, you'll start wondering: "why me?" or "life isn't fair to me." Your anger is a mask for the pain behind it. Your anger might seem endless right now but know that it's a phase that will eventually pass. The more you feel it, the easier it'll get with time, and the quicker you will heal. Your anger knows no bounds. It can go beyond the death of someone. You're angry because you can't understand how this could happen to you. If you're a strong believer in God or any higher power, you start questioning your faith. You start questioning its existence: "Why did he do this to me?" "If he does exist, he would have protected me from this pain." You can be angry at your family, friends, relatives, yourself, and even God. Your rational brain might be aware of how unrealistic your anger is; but, at that moment, your feelings are too intense to understand any reason.

Initially, you feel lost, clueless, and numb, but slowly anger gives you a direction and a structure to your feelings. You now feel something other than just being numb. You might be angry at the doctor, the person who buried your loved one, or the relative who couldn't attend the last rituals. You might be angry at the person who died as well. Rationally, you know that it wasn't their choice to die. However emotionally you blame them for the pain that they have caused you. Suddenly, you have a direction to project your feelings. Anger is the connection that you feel for the tragedy. It's a step ahead of feeling absolutely nothing. We are usually asked to suppress our anger, but anger is just another way of showing the intensity of our emotions. Anger doesn't show our soft side. It socially represents toughness and strength. It might not be justified, but it is more socially acceptable than being vulnerable. It doesn't always have to be an outrage, it could also be passive-aggressive, bitterness, irritability, anxiety, or resentment. After a phase of disconnection and denial, anger helps you feel.

In our daily life, we are asked to hold our anger, take control over it, and suppress it. When you feel you are lost and have no grounding, hold on to your anger. It will give you a sense of being human and feeling emotions. It will bridge the gap of numbness and give you a sense of connection to other people, even if it's just anger. It's the beginning of adjusting to your new reality. People might consider us unapproachable due to our unpredictable emotions—even though we could benefit from some companionship and comfort. How long this phase lasts depends on how you deal with your anger. You could either let yourself completely feel it so that it subsidizes overtime, or you could choose to suppress it.

Bargaining

Once your anger fades away, you're left in a helpless and vulnerable position. It's a way to hold on to any hope or possibility to minimize the pain you're feeling. As humans, we want to be in control of everything that's around us. While you're trying to cope with the loss, you want to be in control of how the situation went. You think of going to any extent or sacrificing anything just to flip the situation in your favor. You will do whatever you can to save your loved ones. You start praying to God, hoping he can change the situation. At least once in your lifetime, you would've said, "God, please just give me this and I will never ask for anything" or "I will visit the temple once a week if she heals." This is Bargaining.

It's always directed to whichever higher power you believe in, to change your current difficulties. You bargain to make a truce for what you want. It's the helpless feeling of not being able to change your situation that makes you feel miserable. If you are anticipating the loss of a loved one or you have already lost someone, then you know you will do anything in your power to get rid of your pain. You'll take any action, promise any words just to get rid of what you're currently feeling. While you're having this internal negotiation, you become lost in the puzzle of "What ifs" or "If only." You're desperate for things to go back to normal, and that's why you start living life on false hopes. Wishing you could've found the tumor at early stages, or not going out for dinner the night of the accident or helping them solve their problems instead of committing suicide. All these bargains are a defense against the pain that you feel for losing someone.

Guilt comes along with feelings of helplessness. You're willing to gain control, even at your own expense. You start blaming yourself for everything that happened. Blaming yourself will eat you up from within. We continue to find faults within ourselves, blame ourselves for not doing things differently, and bargain our current reality for a perceived one (which we are aware is impossible). You start reflecting on your relationship with that person and think about all the things you could have done differently. You would want to change any disconnection, fights, disagreements, or hurt that you've caused. You think about changing all the situations where you've been mean to them. We live in the past and think of how different situations could have been if we had decided to do something about it.

Depression

Depression is a mood disorder that constantly makes you feel sad, unhappy, and uninterested. It's a more subtle and quiet stage. There is no denying or effort for changing the reality. You're no longer running away from your feelings. You realize you cannot run away from your pain and start feeling it abundantly. Our dream world and imaginations have relaxed as we start facing our new reality. You look at your current situation and drown in its misery. Depression is a natural response to grief and is not associated with a mental health condition. You start experiencing the pain and loss that you're suffering. You think that you're going to feel the emptiness forever. That since their existence has ceased to exist, you will never feel normal again.

You take a step back from your daily life and live your days with a fog of sadness. You feel like there's no reason for your existence, or even living your day has become meaningless to you. You refuse to get out of bed, eat or work during the day, or do something that you once enjoyed. You feel the lack of strength to do anything throughout the day. If this stage goes on for long, it can also affect your physical health. You start to lose weight, you don't drink enough water, you have multiple headaches or high blood pressure, and you start getting weaker by the day. It might take a toll on your digestive system as well—you have no accountability for what's happening around, you barely remember anything, or you might be facing trouble going off to sleep. A night of good sleep is necessary for your impeccable health. Your trouble sleeping can affect your hormone levels and mood. It can cause insomnia, sleep depression, or sleep apnea. There are numerous symptoms of depression.

While all of these symptoms are common, not everyone will experience all of them. The symptoms that occur, how often they happen, how long they last, and how severe they depend on the individual. A few symptoms can have a pattern that could be different for everyone. The main reason behind depression is the lack of feel-good chemicals like serotonin and dopamine. These chemicals are called neurotransmitters that aren't functioning the right way because of your trauma. It might go beyond this point and make you feel suicidal. It can be common to have suicidal thoughts when you're grieving the death of your partner or parent. You constantly feel worthless, guilty, and have a pessimistic mindset. There's a lot of self-hatred involved in a few cases. Feeling sad at times is okay. But when it becomes a constant state of being, that's when it reaches clinical depression. In such extreme cases, you need to seek professional help. A counselor or a therapist can help you see beyond your thoughts and navigate your feelings in a way that's comfortable to you. As overwhelming as this stage is, it's necessary for your grieving process. This is an inevitable stage. You cannot skip this in your process.

Acceptance

Acceptance doesn't mean you won't feel the pain. It doesn't mean that you're okay with the death of someone you love. You cannot expect yourself to be joyful. It's okay to never feel the same again. Most people are never okay after losing a mother. Such incidents can change you and your perception of life in general. It's understandable depending on your experience and the way you cope with it. It's more about accepting wholeheartedly the incident that took place. You acknowledge the pain, suffering, and loss. Your emotions have started to stabilize, and you begin to feel sane again.

You're now re-entering your reality. It's a part of your life. You learn new ways to live your current reality. You start molding and adjusting to your new life. You try to live in this new norm where you're okay with missing the deceased one. You might try to resist and not accept the new norm. But eventually, through bits and pieces, you start accepting. You come to terms with the fact that your loved one is not going to come back. You cannot maintain your past life, but you start learning and growing in this new life where you move forward along with your deceased one in your mind, heart, and soul. You start reaching out to your friends and family members at this stage. You're more vocal about the way you're feeling instead of pushing them away out of anger and spite. You start relying on them more, knowing that they want to help you and want what's best for you.

You may also feel that you're going back to another stage before feeling acceptance. It's the most difficult stage, and so it's common for you to go back and forth to different stages before completely accepting your reality. We learn how to fill their shoes in our lives. You start learning and healing the part of your life where they played an important role. We can't restore the loss, but we can meet new people, form new bonds, and have new inter-dependencies. Instead of denying your needs and wants, you find new ways and changes to meet them. You start walking on this unknown path which might be scary at first. But taking one step ahead will help you figure out the next step. You just need to do what feels right at the moment and believe that good things will unfold on your path at the right time.

Initially, David Kessler only wrote the five stages of grief mentioned above in his book, *On Grief and Grieving*. Later, based on his research, hard-earned experience, knowledge, and wisdom, he introduced us to the sixth stage of grief.

Finding Meaning

Various people look for closure after the incident. They believe that they cannot move on without having closure. It's important to find meaning once you've completed the five stages mentioned above. It can transform your grief into a peaceful experience. You cannot have closure while you're dealing with death because that person cannot return, but you walk ahead in life with this experience by your side. So, it's important to turn this grief into something valuable, meaningful, and peaceful.

You can find meaning in the smallest of things. Remember the traditions she used to love and keep them alive. Name family traditions in her honor. You can make a journal of all her happy memories with you or an album of family pictures. You can have a little collection of something that she owned, like a specific pin, which you can keep with you. These things might look small or difficult initially, but eventually, they will bring you a sense of peace. You can use her favorite ring as a necklace, so you never have to feel her absence. She's always with you. If you've gone through a miscarriage, keep the sonogram or the doctor's reports in the memory of your unborn child. You can also hold a charity event, donation, or rescue animals in their memory.

Pick a cause that was personal to her and make a difference in the world. It's a great way to honor her memory and leave a mark on this world on her behalf. It doesn't have to be any huge event, even something as small as feeding stray animals can give you a sense of closeness with her. Take care of things that mattered the most to her. Did she have any plants that she loved or a pet that she looked after? You bring that pet over to your house and look after it. You don't need to let go of the incident or the person. What you need to learn is to remember and cherish them with all the love in your heart. You talk about them with fondness in your words.

Chapter 3:

Dealing With Anger While

Grieving

When you're going through grief, it's natural to feel tired, frustrated, and trapped. When a situation is not in our control, we feel angry, and death is one of those situations. These emotions surface from time to time, and you're looking for an emotional outlet. It could be someone or something. It's the way you feel when you think that the loss you're facing is unjustified. Once you stop denying the loss that has occurred, you start seeing the reality, which makes you feel as if life has been unfair to you. Your mind tries to deflect the pain and that's when you start looking for things and people to blame. You want to be understood when you're going through tragedy. But you cannot expect someone to be understanding without expressing your feelings. You cannot expect people to be mind readers.

Healthily communicating your feelings is essential to access the help that you need in times of grief. If you're a friend or family member of someone who's grieving, you need to understand and be there for them. You cannot assume their needs. Listen intently and ask what they need from you. You can bring more meaning to their life when you do something that they want, rather than doing something that you think they might want. Understanding the cause or reason behind each emotion will be more helpful than just understanding their anger. When you're aware you can keep your expectations in alignment with reality. Take a step back and analyze the entire situation before you react to someone's anger. Understand the reason behind their rage. Whether they are hurt or scared. Instead of replying out of anger, ask them: "What did I do wrong?" A question like this will make them reflect on their actions and help them understand that their rage wasn't justified. It gives them a chance to reflect on their words and actions.

When a close one is grieving for their loss, you are likely to be experiencing anger at some point. You might ask for an explanation, but sometimes their rage will be too immense for them to explain. In such cases, it's best to not take anything seriously. Know that it wasn't a personal attack. Recognize the habits and practices that create unsettling emotions within them. It's easier to help someone when you understand the roots of their problems. You can then help them solve the root cause of their problems. When you're the one suffering from pain and anger, make sure you apologize and mend the relationship. You can start by explaining the cause and reasons behind your rage. Anger stems from troubling thoughts and emotions. Their anger is not always meant to be directed towards us. You might wonder what caused that behavior when you did nothing wrong. You believe that you didn't deserve that, which is true. You might have not done anything wrong. But it's important to understand that even though their anger was directed towards you, it doesn't mean you were the root cause of it.

When someone important to us has died, we feel threatened. It leaves us feeling vulnerable to the hole that their death has caused. You're afraid of how to fill in the role that they played in your life. Anger can be directed towards anyone around us. You might question the person who died, your family, the doctor, or even the spiritual practices that you follow religiously. Anger is a way of defending and protecting yourself from pain. Anger is a way of communicating our fears and demons that we try to hide. It's an act to show others that you aren't weak. There is no particular stage for anger in the grieving process. It moves in and out depending on the person. Don't avoid or suppress it. Bottling up your anger will only lead to a disastrous outburst in the future. Don't try to turn it off or run away from it. Feel all the emotions that you can bear. This will help you go through the grief. Ignoring your emotions, stuffing them, or suppressing them will only leave them unresolved. The more you try to tuck them away, the more you'll feel frustrated. They'll show up in unexpected ways and situations. You'll keep tripping over these emotions till you face them head-on.

Unfortunately, the only way to get over a hard feeling, is to go through it. There's no way around it. Feeling them is the only way to reach acceptance of everything that you're going through. Only when you can accept the emotions, you can start working on them. Identify the core of your anger and what triggers or fuels that emotion. Don't let it mold or shape you. Don't let anger change you. Sometimes you're so lost in anger that it takes control of you instead of the other way around. There's no sense of self-control in any form. It can take you by surprise with what you're capable of doing. The rawness of your anger can cause emotional, mental, and physical disarray in your life. It can be frightening to be consumed by such a destructive emotion. You might fail to recognize yourself especially if you've never experienced extreme emotions before. You know that your rage doesn't define you. But the change of events has temporarily made you feel emotions that you're not used to. In certain situations. You might blame yourself as well. You may wonder, "What have I ever done to deserve this pain?" or "Why am I suffering from this pain." You might remove your frustration on yourself. You might direct the anger and resentment to yourself. You might be scared of what your anger is capable of doing, in case you allow yourself to completely engage in it.

It's important to explore other emotions while dealing with anger. While we are dealing with the rawness of your anger, you might question yourself, "Why am I so angry?" Anger is another coping mechanism for your brain to make sense of the tragedy that has occurred. It's important to realize that your anger is based on another negative emotion. It could be sadness or fear that is the primary emotion that leads you to anger, your secondary emotion.

One way to solve your rage is to understand the initial experience of your anger. Anger is a way of shielding ourselves from the primary emotion. If you don't allow your soul to tangle with your emotions to understand the root cause of it, you will keep facing the same problems. Become more aware of the emotions that are feeding and fueling your anger in grief. Understanding your fears and the ways to solve them can reduce your anger in any situation. Disseminate the hierarchy of your anger to understand how you got there (the primary problem). Once you understand how you got there, don't try to solve your anger, instead understand and eradicate the primary problems, which lead to anger.

Your anger is a form of energy. To be angry, it needs a great source of energy. Once you understand that you'll start realizing its powers. Your "fight or flight" response is resembled by your anger. Anger can be handled in two ways. Either you completely lash out at someone, or you internalize your emotions and bottle them up. When you lash out at someone, which is normally our instinctive reaction, it's to make others feel the way you do. You're forcing them to feel the pain with you. You believe that no one can know or understand the pain you feel from within, so you lash out at them, hoping they will sympathize with you.

The second option is to internalize our emotions. We do that when we are afraid to let out our emotions. Anger is easy to express and show whereas fear is a state of being vulnerable. So, expressing your anger might be easy but you are hesitant to let people in on your vulnerable side. You don't trust the people around you. You're afraid to show others a vulnerable side of you. You don't have a safe space to let out everything that you feel. Another reason you internalize your anger is that you're unaware of what could happen once you lash out. You feel like you won't have any control over what you say or do. You would be exposing a side of you that you struggle to manage. You could choose to do either, but the result would be the same drowning emotions that will leave you feeling unstable.

Acting out of anger or completely suppressing it will not end up solving your conflict. Give your anger the reverence that it deserves. It's a fundamental part of the grieving process. Leaving it undone can leave you with unresolved anger, which will then erupt as rage. It creates an atmosphere of chaos within you that will keep growing and eventually drain you. Asking yourself the difficult questions and facing its solution will be the only way to eventually get out of the situation—and being aware of the root cause is the first step to dissolving your anger. Your initial part of discovering the underlying emotions behind your anger is done. The lack of power to change the situation or the trauma that it caused you is directly related to the helplessness that you feel. It might be helpful to find a safe space that can help you express your emotions without any judgments.

You can also find different ways to channel your anger. Some people find their release through physical activities such as sports, intense forms of exercise, a simple run, or a walk. Exercising releases endorphins, which help you boost your mood. While some people might have a creative outlet—such as dancing, writing, painting, or singing, which can help them cope healthily—you can also try writing a letter to the person who died expressing all you feel. Express your anger or sadness, you can shout at them, and hopefully, forgive them for leaving you behind. It will help you explore and examine the ways your fear has left you feeling immobilized. If your anger is obsessive and you have the desire to inflict physical pain on yourself or others, this is not normal even while grieving. In such cases, it's recommended to seek professional help. To make an appointment with someone who can guide you through your grief and eliminate any chances of danger. Letting go of the anger doesn't mean you're forgetting the person. When you let go of the anger, you start seeing the world.

All these emotions tend to release stress hormones in your body. This creates a significant amount of physical changes in your body. The need for oxygen in your body increases. Your sugar levels, heart rate, and blood pressure are high. Your muscles become tense. The chances of a blood clot occurring anywhere in your body also increase. It also lowers your immunity so you're more likely to catch a cold or flu. Grief can also cause joint pain, headaches, or back pain. The stress hormones can stun your muscles when they come in contact. You might find comfort in food during times of stress like many others. Due to anxious feelings, it's difficult for your stomach to digest the food you eat. You might face digestive issues depending on your food habits as well. These physical changes can increase the risk of a heart attack or stroke. The way your body reacts is individualistic. You might experience none of these symptoms, all of them, or just a combination of a few. There's no guide to it. It's how your body decides to react.

Sometimes your anger can turn inwards in the form of guilt. This usually happens when you're tired of blaming everything and everyone around you. You don't want to feel anger anymore, so you blame yourself for either causing it (even if you haven't) or not preventing it. You feel like you could have done much more. As if you weren't enough in that situation.

For example, you were avoiding arguing with your mother before she left for work, and then she met with a car accident and died on the spot. You blame yourself for the accident. You believe that she was probably driving in anger because of your arguments, and that's why she couldn't concentrate while driving. You believe that her irresponsibility was caused by you. You take the entire blame on yourself and refuse to believe that it was her fault or the other driver's fault for causing the accident. You try coming up with different alternatives and solutions for what you could have done instead of yelling at her before she left. "I should have," "I could have," or "If only" become popular phrases in your vocabulary. All the guilt and despair are drowning you and you feel completely lost.

Although this phase can look more guilty than anger, this guilt gives birth to anger that's directed towards you. There's no logical reason for blaming yourself.

None of your thoughts can change your actions in the past. You cannot go back and change what you've already done. This sense of helplessness builds on your frustration. The built-up of this frustration then leaves you with full-blown rage. Not being able to change the situation makes you feel worthless. Children and teens tend to be angrier than adults as they do not have the maturity to reason or understand everything around them.

Losing my mother at the age of 14 brought a lot of hurt and anger. I was mad at my father for not being able to do anything, I was mad at the doctors for not saving my mother, and I was mad at the relative who told me, "At least she's no longer suffering" or that "You saw it coming, so move on with your life." No one understood how difficult it was to see my mother pass away in pain. To see her attached with tubes and wires for so many months. The only question that kept me haunted was, "Why me?" There was no definite answer to it. But that didn't stop me. For the longest time, I didn't know why I deserved the death of my mother. It kept me awake at night and distracted during the day.

When I finally realized that I wasn't getting any answer to my question, I turned to alcohol. I wasn't ready to face my feelings, I was angry that no one had any answers to what I was going through. I kept myself distracted by consuming alcohol. Weekend parties as a teenager had become my thing. To others, it looked like a normal teenage thing to do. A phase that everyone goes through. When in reality, it was the only form of distraction from what I was feeling. I was using alcohol as my crutch to keep me going. This went on for a few years. I got into a university and continued my studies. One day, I found myself in a terrible situation due to my drinking habits. I found myself in a "Drunk tank" and knew at that moment something had to change.

The weeks that followed after that incident wasn't easy. That incident pushed me to make the change that I had prolonged for so many years. It didn't come easy. I was on the verge of dropping out. That's when I shifted my energy and focus from alcoholism to working out in the gym. It was like a true savior. I started building habits that I was aware would benefit me. Consciously choosing what's right for me was the beginning of my healing journey. After years of drowning in my pain, anger, and sadness, I was finally ready to talk about all that was going on. I was around 20 at this point, and I knew I had to change. I started reading books that spoke about self-help, self-development, and grief in general. These books helped me believe that I wasn't alone—that there are thousands of people going through this every day. So, if they could overcome it, then so can I. They gave me the knowledge I needed to shift my mindset and grow. I understood how important it was to not only be aware of the way you feel, but to also talk about it. It was painful at first, but the more I spoke about it, the less angry I got.

The pain started depleting and it became normal for me to talk about my mother's death. It still hurts to believe that my mother is no longer with me, but I'm also aware that carrying that pain only makes me stronger and more resilient. I took it slow, one small step at a time. I developed these habits over the years, and then the year 2020 came along. It was the year that made everyone reflect on their inner self. During the 2020 lockdown, everyone had to isolate themselves. Being alone with yourself for so many months brought up emotions that we have been suppressing. We could no longer run away from our feelings, and the only option was to face it, whether you liked it or not. I was no different than the rest. Although I had built some great habits that helped me cope, I still avoided addressing what I felt from within.

During this lockdown, I experienced some uneasiness. I was in a committed relationship with a woman I dearly loved but couldn't open up to. I believe that I had this deep-rooted fear of someone leaving my life again. That fear was holding me back in my relationship. I was always one foot in and one foot out, which left me at a crossroads. At this point, I was left with two options, either open up and heal my trauma or never be the best version of myself in a relationship. I knew I didn't want to spend the rest of my life in a barely fulfilling relationship. So, I did what I thought was best for me to heal, I joined therapy.

It was the last missing piece to cope with my mother's death. It took me years to join therapy because of the stigma behind it. All these years I thought I had healed and didn't need therapy. I was successful on the outside and that's what mattered. As long as I was doing well with myself, I didn't need therapy—at least that's what I was taught. The stigma around not needing therapy because nothing looked wrong in my life is something that held me back. It's the way you feel that should be the deciding factor in therapy. Don't let the stigma hold you back. Don't believe other's opinions on whether you should take therapy or not. Therapy is extremely personal, and you should be the only deciding factor for it. I believe that these habits helped me through my worst times, but therapy was the last missing piece to get over my emotional turmoil.

Once I started, my therapist recommended I face and relive my trauma through writing everything that happened and the way I feel. That is also what inspired me to write my book. It's not only a means to help someone, but it's also therapeutic for me. When I started, I wrote everything in detail. The time when my mother fell sick, struggles through chemotherapy, last few days, funeral, the things I wish I had told her, and her negative traits. When I started reliving my trauma in detail, I could tell which points were still hurting me. Those were the unhealed parts of me that still needed some healing. Those unhealed parts of me were affecting my current life and the relationships that I was trying to build. This allowed me to see my trauma from a level that I never experienced. Once I let out everything in my notepad, it felt as if a huge weight was lifted off my chest. I knew that the past had no control over me anymore. It stopped hurting me and I could continue living in my present life, without looking over my shoulder.

Some tips will help you through your angry phase:

- **Understand That You're Not Being Yourself**

  Don't let your anger define you. You know that you've not always been this way, and it's the situation that has caused this reaction out of you. Don't let your anger mold you into a different person. For someone calm and patient, you might find it abnormal to have an extreme reaction. It's normal to have an abnormal reaction (anger) to an abnormal situation (death). It's easier for some people to be angry than sad. You're waiting for all of this to be a dream so that you can finally go back to your reality where everything is the same. No one has died or is in a hospital bed and you're in the same happy space as before. There will be someday when you feel like you've overcome the anger, and then a few days where you're completely consumed by it. It's an ongoing process that has a few good and bad days.

- **Express It**

  It's important to express our anger but healthily. It's so easy to just lash out and remove all the frustration. That might feel good at that moment, but it can be extremely damaging and hurtful to the person on the receiving end of it. This might be tough but take a moment before you decide to speak in anger. It's hard to not let your feelings blind your judgments. With practice, though, you can get there. In some cases, you're tempted to put on a smiling and happy face because people depend on you for support and comfort. You feel the burden of responsibilities on your shoulder. When you're the eldest in your family, you have kids or younger siblings who look up to you. You feel the need to guide them and make sure their emotional and materialistic needs are met. That there's no hole or gap left by the sudden death of a person.

While you're trying to meet someone's requirements, you tend to forget your own. In such times, you unknowingly repress your emotions. You know you can't afford to look weak. In such cases, even though you aren't expressing your feelings, it might show in the smallest of ways. Anything small can put you off. You're lashing out on the smallest of inconveniences. You're more short-tempered than usual. You're bound to scream at the smallest of things just because you don't have another emotional outlet. If you want to scream, it's okay. Shout or yell at the heavens for taking someone away from you. Just make sure you're screaming at home or in a car and not at somebody else. Make a safe space.

Another form of letting out your angry emotions can be writing a letter. Remove all your anger, say all that you want to say, and just put out any words that come to mind. It doesn't have to make sense to you or anyone else as long as it's serving its purpose. Even though you're performing your daily tasks, you're unable to live in the moment. You're doing what you have to do, but you're struggling to do it with complete conviction which is normal. Even though you need to keep your calm for others, you can find healthy ways to cope with your anger.

Don't neglect yourself for others' needs. You need the same support as others. So, make space for yourself and take care of your own emotional needs. There's no restriction on how you can or should express your feelings. Even crying out of anger is a reasonable solution. Don't do something just out of social acceptance. Express your anger the way it comes to you. Allow your body to decide the way it wants to express itself. Don't force yourself or stop yourself from crying because of gender stereotypes. You might not allow yourself to cry in front of your kids but it's okay to have a breakdown or cry to someone you trust. When you're at a mature age, you might have a handful of people who you can blindly trust. Let that be your safe space as you try to navigate your life.

If tears come naturally to you, it's your body's way to release anger, sadness, pain, and hurt. It cleanses all the pent-up emotions. A good cry can later make you feel lighter and fresher than before. In the age of social media, it's easy to get distracted by fake positivity. The only way to feel positive is to go through each negative emotion and feel them till they start dissolving. Not everyone has it in them to face their negative side without any distraction. That's why there are so many people who are unhealed and traumatized by something that happened to them years ago. They don't let their tears heal their hearts. People often say, "Sorry, I didn't mean to cry. I know I look weak." This stems from parents and family members that are uncomfortable with emotions. Crying helps heal depression, anxiety, or any tough emotions. Going through those uneasy days is a sign of courage, strength, and bravery.

- **Find Freedom in Forgiveness**

Why should you forgive someone when you're hurt? You didn't do anything wrong; you're hurting because someone died. You have all the right to be angry or unhappy. So what is the need for your forgiveness? Forgiving a person or a situation will break any baggage that it holds over you. The freedom from that baggage will heal you in ways nothing else can. Doesn't matter who was responsible for your pain, they have caused you the loss that you're suffering, or they have intentionally wronged you.

Forgiveness is not for them but for your inner peace, healing, and growth. Even anger binds you emotionally to something that you blame. It weighs you down and increases the burden on you. Forgiving is not about disconnecting yourself from the incident but letting go of anything that doesn't serve you well. Instead of hating or being angry at the doctor, you choose to forgive them, so you can move on without any hate in your heart. Forgiving someone is one thing, but you also need to ask for forgiveness.

It's from those who you've intentionally or unintentionally hurt in your grieving process. The friends or family members that you might have mistreated or the times when you've lashed out on someone innocent. Apologizing and clarifying your behavior can restore and heal any damage that you might have caused to the person or the relationship that you share with them. Acknowledging and accepting your flaws will help you repair the relationships and yourself. The burden of a loved one's death is enough, you don't need to add irrelevant arguments to further your misery.

- **Analyze the Righteousness of Your Anger**

The things you say or do out of anger are not always right. Sometimes you need to take a pause and analyze from a logical standpoint whether your demands are valid. You could be asking for anything, an explanation, more money, property, or anything else, but the basis on which you're asking for these things isn't valid. Your anger makes you illogical sometimes. The death of your loved ones makes you so angry that you try creating problems in everything that happens around you. While it's understandable from a psychological perspective, it's not justified or fair to anyone around you. While you lash out and demand anything that you want out of anger. Try taking a pause and analyze the reason behind your demands. Does it come out of genuine need or just out of ego and anger?

Chapter 4:

Ways You Can Support

Yourself

Showing Kindness

Showing kindness is the first step to support yourself. Going through the stages of grief is emotionally, mentally, and physically exhausting. It's important to offer yourself kindness, love, and patience. Kindness is the best gift you can give to those who you love. Love yourself enough to show kindness and empathy towards yourself. It's to be kind and compassionate to yourself. It's the same thing that you would do for a friend. Listen to yourself rant and grieve, buy yourself some food, offer to get yourself something, and show yourself all the compassion that you can have. You need to learn how to befriend yourself.

Start where you are right now. Is your house clean? Are you still eating take-out that you bought two days ago? Are you ignoring any social events? When was the last time you showered? Are you constantly consuming alcohol or have an addiction to any substances? Allow yourself to begin with one thing at a time. Don't burden yourself with everything around you. You might be the kind of person who has constant restless energy who needs to work or do something at all times. You always have a tight schedule. There are people constantly relying on you if you're the head of the family or you run a business. You have multiple roles and obligations to fulfill so you're constantly bottling up your emotions.

Consider taking a break for yourself. To rest and rejuvenate. Make your schedule slow and include some small breaks in it. Sit and enjoy your favorite music, go for a walk, or just watch your favorite movie. Address your inner critic or judgments who shame you for crying too much or not enough. Quit calling yourself names for not doing enough. You have these completely unrealistic expectations out of yourself that no sane man can match up to. Grieving takes up a lot of your energy so don't burden yourself with expectations. You're trying your best and that's an achievement in itself. You're not a wimp or a loser for not checking off everything on your to-do list.

Pause and listen to these noises in your head. Drop constantly putting yourself down and just be and feel grief for as long as you can. Embracing vulnerability, anxiousness, and irritability is normal for someone who's experiencing separation or loss. Be tender so you can understand your needs and requirements during this phase of hardships. It's a part of you so there's no need to hide or tuck it away.

Embrace all the "bad" sides of you with all the love possible. Realize how normal it is to just be sad. We experience polarity as humans and these emotions help us grow and build for a life that we can't even imagine yet. Acknowledge all that you do for yourself and be grateful for all of it. Express gratitude for all the small steps that you've taken for yourself, the days you've gone out of your comfort to do something nice and healthy, comforting yourself when you've spent a day in bed just crying and moping, and for providing even the smallest bit of happiness for yourself.

Meditation

The pain that you're surrounded by is the closest thing to your heart. It tries to guard your heart against any other pain by building a wall of stone. The pain denies any change that comes your way. It makes sure you're unable to love, mourn, or be loved by anyone else. The feeling of pain lingers even after you're done mourning. You'll continue to suffer till you don't stop running away from these emotions. The power of leaning into your pain is so strong that you'll start building a friendship with it. Name and acknowledge all that you've been through. Instead of letting it create a wall of stone outside, let it in your heart. The pain of grief will start warming up to you. Instead of shutting out the world, you'll welcome new feelings and experiences in your heart. You start living life with an open heart. Feeling each of your emotions will heal you to live with an open heart.

But you may wonder, how do you feel the emotions that you've locked up in the deepest corner of your heart? One of the best ways to heal yourself is meditation. You don't have to sit every day like a yogi for 45 minutes. It's okay to start small. You can start with something called mindful meditation. It's a basic meditation where you concentrate only on your breath. The idea is to simply sit in one place and feel each breath going in and out of your body. You'll feel unique sensations with each breath as you inhale and exhale. Find a comfortable corner in your house where you're sitting on the floor or chair. Try to keep a fixed spot for your daily meditation practice. It will eventually make you more comfortable. You can sit down in Indian style, on a couch, a cushion, or even a bed, whatever makes you most comfortable.

Now, you might think it's so easy to just sit and breathe. But what most people don't realize is that as humans we are programmed to constantly think. The next idea, suggestion, or thing to do. You're thinking about how you need to clean the dishes, finish the last two tasks on your to-do list, call back your friend, reply to an important email, or the dress you'll wear for tomorrow's dinner.

Your mind is constantly wondering about the future of repeating the past in your mind. It's never without a thought and that's what contributes to your anxiety. It's okay and normal for your mind to wander during the beginning stages of meditation. What you need to do is notice. Notice every time your mind wanders off to some thought and gets it back to your breath. It's normal for people to not be able to sustain their attention after one or two breaths.

Don't judge yourself for the thoughts that occur. Just simply be aware of them and let it go. Judging them will lead to feeling the cool air that you're breathing and the way your lungs and stomach inflate with each breath. Initially, all you'll be doing is bringing your attention to your breath before it wanders off again. As you feel your body relaxing, you can hear your heartbeat as well. With practice, you'll find yourself naturally just focusing on the breath. This will offer you the peace and calmness that you've struggled to feel since the tragedy that occurred in your life.

If you're someone who has more restless energy you're likely to struggle with meditating in one corner. You have a scattered mind that's difficult to tame. There's still hope for similar people. This is not the only form of meditation that exists. Walking meditation might suit you better. In walking meditation, your attention is on the way you walk instead of your breath. Walk at a slow pace and feel every step that you take. Keep a soft gaze at the floor and keep your attention on the ground. Notice the way your legs feel as you take one step at a time. This is not meant to be an exercise, so walk short distances. Breathe in as you take a step and breathe out with another step. be aware of the way your foot touches the ground, your heels to toes. Slowly turn around as you reach the corner to slowly return to your starting point. Be relaxed and continue the attention till the end of your meditation session. It's on you to decide which meditation is meant for you.

Irrespective of the approach you select, just remember the initial stage of meditation is hard. Don't be discouraged by the lack of your attention span. It's normal to take weeks or even months before you begin to get the hang of it. Once you do, all those days of struggle will be worth it. You could seek some external assistance to guide you in your initial days. There are a lot of guided meditations that you can access online. There are various books written for it and a few people take either online or offline classes to meditate. I would personally recommend an online class because not only will an experienced teacher guide you, but also a class will be fixed on your schedule, so your chances of skipping a session will be reduced by a great percentage.

Meditation can be extremely challenging and hard to pursue. So, why are we putting ourselves through such difficulties in our already existing tough situations? We are trying to pursue something unnatural to us, so it's important to understand the reason behind it. The primary reason for meditating is to calm and steady your mind. You focus on one domain only. Your mind is so busy thinking about every little detail about everything around you. Your mind is all over the place.

When you focus on your breath, you gather all the attention on one domain which allows your mind to take a break from all the racing thoughts in your mind.

You feel more composed and centered. As your mind calms down, you start focusing on each of your five senses. Not just smell, touch, or taste, but you even begin to experience and explore your mind and body. The way you breathe, thoughts, and emotions as well. It's a complete and wholesome experience of who you are. Mindfulness meditation will help you divert your attention from the past or future to your reality. It's about focusing on what's happening right now.

When you're completely living in your present, it allows you to pause and focus on your thoughts. You develop deep insight into what and how you think or feel. When you have the opportunity to analyze your thoughts, you take the power away from your mind. With regular practice, you can respond wisely and empathetically to anything that is happening. Instead of your mind being in control of what and how you think, you get to choose the way you want to control your mind. A few tips for walking mindfully are to choose a place that's indoors which is comfortable and big enough for you. Even if you have to choose outdoors, make sure there's a minimal disturbance. Take on a full breath in with one step and a full breath out with another step.

Your awareness should be on the feet that's touching the ground with each breath. This might be awkward at first, which is why indoor walking meditation is recommended so you don't feel awkward or overthink about the way others look or think about you. Set your timer for two to five minutes for any type of meditation. In any form of meditation, don't try to go beyond five minutes as a beginner unless it naturally comes to you. People struggle to meditate even for two minutes in the initial stages so it's okay. Focus on the sounds around you or the way your fingers are feeling. Notice and be in touch with every sensation in and around you, without any labels or judgments of whether you like it or not.

Mindfulness as a Way of Living

People are suffering from grief because they continue to live in their past. I'm not asking you to forget your past but stop reliving it constantly in your mind. It only adds more to your pain, suffering, and anxiety. You need to start living in your present more than your past. It's okay to think about your past, but don't make that your lifestyle. You give away complete control over your present to the events in your past. Mindfulness is not just a type of meditation, but also a way of living. We are constantly living in autopilot mode. Reflecting on our past experiences or worrying about the events that will take place in the future. But we are rarely ever attentive to our present. We are just moving along with our lives without completely experiencing the depth or meaning of it.

This happens because we are living in our minds and not in our reality. This might be a completely new experience and although it looks simple, it's not easy. It's a profound yet difficult way of living. As you practice it, you maintain a non-judgmental, kind, peaceful, and loving way of the way you feel. Mindfulness has the value of being candid and openhearted. The intention behind practicing mindfulness is to create a safe and welcoming space for your unhealed emotions and imperfect self that a good friend would do for you. An essential quality of mindfulness is being non-judgmental. You have to let go of all judgments and labels when you're being mindful, whether you like it or not. It helps you create a safe space for all the emotions you experience in grief.

Mindfulness can be practiced beyond meditation as well. You don't need to do anything special about it. The beauty of mindfulness is that you can incorporate it into the smallest activity of your daily life. Mindfulness is about drawing all your attention to the way your senses are reacting, as well as your emotions and thoughts to everything around you. Notice the thoughts that are currently in your mind without any judgments or labels. Be aware of your emotions and the way you're feeling right now—notice the way your soap bubbles up when you're washing the dishes, the taste of the food you're eating, the smell of your body wash, or just the sight of the mountains in front of you. Being present and experiencing every tiny emotion will take you away from whatever it is that's bothering you. You can practice this while driving, running, eating, or working.

The intention is to bring your body and mind together at the same time and place (present). Little by little, you'll slowly notice the way you acknowledge, grasp, hold, and enjoy pleasant experiences and disregard unpleasant experiences. You'll become aware of your shortcomings. The pain points and struggles in your life that you could work on, and the unnecessary suffering because of your overthinking habits. You start becoming naturally more mindful, and it leads to a freeway of living life. One on your terms and conditions.

Practicing mindfulness situations filled with suffering and grief, you will experience the event as it is. Sometimes we make the event bigger than it is. We overthink ideas, situations, and people in our minds that don't exist in our reality. We hype up the event with 100 different "what ifs," which only adds to our suffering. There's no reason to suffer for something that doesn't exist in our reality. We look at everything in its original form, as it is. The safe space you've created is to hold all your emotions and experiences, even if you don't like them.

For example, if you're going through your phase of anger, try to sit with your emotions irrespective of how uncomfortable it can get for you. When you sit with your emotions without any preconceived notions, it gives you the space to dig deeper and explore more of what you feel and the underlying emotions. Anger is a mask for vulnerability, and the only way you can experience or explore your vulnerability is by taking time to feel your emotions even if it's challenging. Take one day at a time and hold your emotions tenderly. You don't need to make yourself feel rushed through your emotions, take them as they come.

Your healing process will happen over some time and not overnight. It helps us find the strength to deal with our suffering and loss. The way you deal with your loss is personal. But mindfulness is a guide to making the space you need to deal with your grief. Eating mindfully is extremely beneficial for your mental and physical health. Put away all your electronic gadgets. Sit with some food in a place that's quiet and peaceful. Minimal distractions will help you focus on the meal kept in front of you. Focus all your attention on the food, the smell, texture, color. Eat slowly and chew your food properly. Feel the taste of it and let it linger in your mouth for a few minutes. This will help your mind to calm down and also, allow your food to properly digest without any distractions. Each meal that's eaten mindfully will help you grow mentally and physically. It promotes better digestion, and you'll eat the right quantity. You end up overeating when you're too distracted with your thoughts and emotions. Eating mindfully strikes a good balance. Being mindful is a way of listening to your deeper voices and connecting with your vulnerabilities and strengths.

Get in Touch With Your Roots

We live in a paradox. Different elements of the new fast-paced culture exhaust our connection to the natural world. Human beings are naturally drawn to build a connection with different life forms. The prosperity of our existence depends on other creatures. Yet, as we get prosperous we drift away from the natural world. Parents these days struggle to get their kids away from their pads and laptops. They try to get their kids outdoors, but the kids refuse to get dirty in sand or mud. Gardens and playtime are no longer attractive for kids because of these immersive technologies. Wanting to be indoors and constantly watch their cartoons and play on their pads. As adults, we are constantly working on our laptops or watching Netflix.

When you go outdoors, you're constantly on your phone updating your social media, clicking pictures, navigating roads, replying to an email, tweeting something, meeting deadlines, or listening to music. Without your phone, you feel handicapped. When we experience a major loss, it's important to go back to the basics. Nature can help you heal in ways you didn't think you could. It doesn't have to be the Himalayas or deep in some woods. Even the park next to you or your backyard can make you feel more connected. Even if you can't go outside, just look at the sky from your window. Being in nature is so effortless. Just looking at the clouds in the sky, watching the water in a river or ocean, hearing the birds chirp, or feeling the grass under your feet. Nature draws us in without asking for anything in return. There's nothing to do except you effortlessly watch, feel, and observe everything around you.

"Being in nature one becomes aware of the infinite circle of life," Dr. Kirsti A. Dyer tells Mother Nature Network. "There is evidence of decay, destruction, and death; there are also examples of rejuvenation, restoration, and renewal. The never-ending cycle of birth, life, death, and rebirth can put life and death into perspective and impart a sense of constancy after experiencing a life-changing loss or a death." (Lambiase, 2013). Coping with someone's death can be an emotionally draining process. Connecting with nature can help troubled individuals to look beyond their grief and pain. Outdoor places can be your haven during despair. Going in nature can also help you go down the memory lane of your childhood. The first time you went biking, going to the park with your parents, or swimming in the lake on a family vacation. Some of us love solitude, instead of loneliness, you build a connection with nature. You can include various activities in nature as well. Hiking, swimming, camping, picnic, gardening, biking, fishing or even walking your dog. It will keep you entertained and rejuvenated. When you return from nature, you're more focused, you get inspired to be creative and your cognitive thinking improves. It helps with your grief and even after that.

A Cycle of Positivity

Create a positive cycle for yourself. Our brain has a negative bias due to the genetics of our ancestors. Our earliest ancestors used to scan any situation looking for threats to stay alive. They used to fight wildlife and other humans to survive in the forests. In today's life, we are not required to fight lions, and yet the susceptibility to remember and hold onto negative experiences lives in us. Negative events and experiences are stuck to us like glue and paint a picture of the way we look at everything in and around us. Even the memories of our childhood are more likely to be negative. Like the time you fell off a bike, you had a bad dentist appointment, the injections that you had to take, getting into a fight, or any arguments at home.

We might not remember every detail, but we are more likely to remember the more hurtful and embarrassing memories of our past. The more positive events and experiences are either taken for granted or forgotten. You're less likely to remember times when your mom surprised you with your favorite cake or your friends surprised you for your birthday. You hardly register them in your thoughts and memories.

You lack gratitude for all the good things in your past. It takes an active presence of mind and practice to shift your mindset to be more positive. Your subconscious mind affects 95 percent of your life. The way you perceive your life stems from the wiring of your subconscious mind. It's our subconscious mind that holds a long history of all the insights, beliefs, memories, feelings, and experiences. To change the way we live, we need to change the way we perceive everything around us. The perception of our reality is based on our deeply rooted beliefs.

The Beliefs of Your Subconscious Mind

Your beliefs are the roots of your life. Although it doesn't change the situation that we are currently dealing with, we can change our perspective towards it. First, you need to understand that your subconscious mind will hold onto things that you consistently feed it. So, if you're constantly telling yourself that the grief is bigger than you or that you will never be able to move on from the death of a loved one, then that's what you'll experience. Become aware of all your limiting beliefs. The ones that hold you back or make you feel worse about a situation.

Your unpleasant present behavior will always have a negative belief behind it. These negative beliefs act as a hindrance to adapting to your new reality. Self-motivation is the key to moving on from grief. You need to have strong intent and challenge all the beliefs that are stopping you from moving on. You cannot change the fact that someone you deeply loved has passed away, but you need to shift your focus from their death to the memories you have with them and the memories that you can make in your present and future. Life doesn't stop for anyone, and this doesn't imply that you forget them. Remember them in times of need and keep them close to your heart as you move on with your journey.

Once you isolate your limiting beliefs, you can incorporate new behaviors and routines that can help you cope with your current reality. Remember that the subconscious mind only picks up those behaviors which are repeated consistently. You cannot expect a complete change of direction by just doing something nice only once. You'll gently notice a shift from a negative to a positive side as you keep working on your inner self. For your subconscious mind to cope, it requires 100 percent of your commitment. Your desire to truly change will not be easy. It's not a commitment of a few days or weeks. Your patience through this process is one of the key elements. If you lose your patience, you'll go back to page one. So, know that it's okay to take as much time as you need.

It takes months of talking to yourself, which you already do (even though you're unaware of it) and picturing accurately what you want from your life. Your subconscious mind will take in everything that you say, show, or do. It doesn't have the power to recognize and reject anything good or bad. The words, actions, and feelings that you focus on will amplify in your life. So, you need to start by promising yourself that you will not pay attention to any thought or action that doesn't deserve it. Talking to yourself is the thought that runs in your mind. You need to change the narrative. Initially, it might feel wrong, or fake. You find it difficult to identify or relate to any kind of positivity. But as you start talking to yourself with more kindness, patience, and empathy, your narrative will start going in a more positive direction.

Before something reaches you at a subconscious level, it goes through your conscious mind first. Your conscious mind is the place where your thoughts breed. It has the power to accept or reject any thought, idea, or behavior. Your conscious mind will accept what seems like reality to you. So, if you say, "I am no longer affected by the death of my mother," it will reject the thought because you know you are affected by the situation. When a thought is rejected by a conscious mind, it will fail to sink into your subconscious mind. So, even when you're trying to change your train of thought, make it realistic and believable.

One single thought will not change your reality. But it's the repetition of the thought that will eventually bring change in your life. The choice to make your life better will challenge your patience. When you're trying to shift your focus, pay minimal attention to the things that you don't want. You need to have a clear-cut image of what you want. Be as specific with the details of the life that you want to live.

Create a master plan of all the major milestones that you want to accomplish. Then create a plan with all the ways that you can accomplish each of those milestones. Visualize the details of the plan over and over again. For example, if your father has expired, imagine yourself analyzing his assets and liabilities. What are his remaining debts and which assets are you taking over? Bills that you need to pay off on behalf of your father. Do you want to live in your father's house or sell it to someone? Make those decisions and believe that every decision will have the best results. Play out the decisions in your mind, the way it has created a positive impact for you and everyone around you as well. Imagining this at least once a day will rewire your subconscious mind.

We are always jumping to conclusions. But why are those conclusions always negative? You get nothing out of imagining negative conclusions except unhappiness. Instead, think of all the good things that can happen for you, through just one decision. Along with imagining, another essential tool is to create affirmative sentences in your narrative. Speaking of your desires in your present tense will sink into your subconscious mind. For example, sentences such as: "I am strong enough to get through these troubling situations." These statements are not only positive but also realistic which will be easy for your conscious and subconscious mind to believe. Make up more statements that are meaningful and specific to you. Remember, repetition is the key.

Many people practice this regularly by writing down their affirmations. Practicing them in the morning will set a good tone for the day or at night so that you sleep on a peaceful thought. The simplicity of this idea does not reflect the massive change it can bring over time. You create new thoughts and a new direction for yourself. The repetition will gradually bring a change in your perception and attitude. Focus on feeling your affirmations whenever you repeat them. Believe that you are strong and are capable of solving crises.

Your faith in the affirmations will create the change you desire. Change your actions to support your affirmations. Even the smallest victory should be celebrated to encourage your progress. All this inner communication is under your control, and that will change the way you look at everything around you. You make peace with situations that are out of your control by working on your inner self to change your perception. You change so that you can adapt to the situation and make the most out of it. Everyone possesses inner wisdom.

All you need to do is tap into that wisdom that will help you cope with any loss that you're going through. You can receive all the external help that you need, but only when you start working on yourself, you'll heal in the best possible way. Everyone possesses the ability to grow, including you.

Turning Pain Into Passion

We all have heard of people who work extremely hard after a major accident or loss that they have suffered. They are the courageous ones that transform their pain into passion. Their pain acts as guidance to help those who are suffering the same trauma or tragedy. They devote themselves to a cause. It leads to building a community that helps one another to cope with similar situations.

Certain unspeakable losses have brought remarkable changes in our society. For example, Mathew Shepard was brutally killed in October 1998 in Laramie, Wyoming for being a part of the LGBTQIA+ community. The death deeply affected his parents, who later became strong advocates of the LGBTQIA+ community. They played an important role in helping the rest of the community to pass a federal law called the Hate Crimes Prevention Act.

There are lots of people who make something out of their grief. It's a way to honor your pain and sufferings. It doesn't always have to be something big, even small changes can have similar effects. For me, writing this book is a way to honor my mother and the pain that I suffered due to her death.

Chapter 4:

Ways You Can Support

Yourself (II)

Journaling

Journaling is an experience that's valuable to cope with your emotions and feelings. You can start a journal that's specific for your grief or even a regular journal for your daily use. There are no rules for journaling, of course, a few techniques that can guide you, but it's your choice. You can journal with pen and paper, on your phone, or any other application. However you decide to keep your journal, it's your safe space to write and say anything that's on your mind. Journaling can be of different types. One where you just dump everything that's on your mind, you can keep a track of things that triggers your anxiety, you can write some memories of the person that's deceased, you can use it as a method to explore your emotions, or you can just write about everything that's happening in your life. There's no fixed step-by-step process. It's what comes naturally from you.

When you're not ready to 'speak it out,' journaling can be an effective way to replace that. You can write it out in your journal, without your emotions overpowering you. You're exploring your emotions while still being in control. You discover and understand the meaning of your grief when you're journaling. When you understand the roots and meaning of your grief, it's easier to deal with it, as opposed to just suppressing it. You can also use this method to move on from your loss/unexpected change.

Writing about these tough times is like a self-narrative that could leave you feeling emotional. In Fact, it's natural to cry when you're letting it out. It's your body's way to relieve any emotions that are causing you distress and pain. Writing without any goals, plans, or previous thoughts is your version of thinking out loud. It's up to you whether you want to share anything out of it or not. It's the most judgment-free zone that you could ever have which makes it a safe space for your innermost fears, emotions, and thoughts to surface. This helps clear your mind and free you up from space and blockages in your mind. Writing down memories can help you remember more happy days than sad ones. It brings a sense of gratitude for all those days that you've spent laughing. Instead of fearing that you lost them and eventually you'll forget and move on, you can write their memories for future reference and safeguard your relationship with them. Recording your journey of grief in a journal can help you keep a track record of where you're at, emotionally and mentally. The grieving journey is a slow process, so sometimes it might feel like you're not making any progress. That's when you start reading the track record you've made, and you'll realize how far you've come. There are multiple ways you can use a journal but doing what makes you feel relaxed is the main aim of it. You can use this method to figure out what your new life is going to be like. Start writing down details that you want or expect out of this new phase and plan out a way to achieve all those things. Figure out how you can make the most out of your worst situation.

Many of us have been told that we do not have the creative skills to write well. Maybe some tutor said that in school or a parent that said when you scored low in your essay. You've believed that you're incapable of writing well. That you're not good enough to write. You're incapable of writing or putting across your feelings and thoughts in words. In that case, throw all of your worries out of the window. You don't need to be a creative writer to be expressive. This is not a piece of art. You aren't expected to make it fancy or artistic. This is about expressing and discovering your innermost feelings.

You write what you think in any language that's comfortable for you. It doesn't have to be the perfect grammar or spelling. It could be broken English for all I care. Your focus should be on your feelings and not your writing style. If you find it difficult to write initially, it's understandable. Maybe you could start by just writing down the emotions that you feel. Happy, sad, angry, just name it. Once you get a little comfortable with it, maybe you could begin describing each of these feelings in detail.

If you're a beginner or just trying this for the first time, start small. Begin with some sentences or just a small paragraph. You could set a timer to let your thoughts flow freely for a few minutes. The best way to start is just to sit with blank paper and pen and see what naturally comes to you. Don't get into it with any preconceived notions and let your instinct guide you. Just write whatever comes to your mind. Sit for however long you can. It can be two or twenty minutes. If at some point you feel it's enough, you're tired, or there's nothing else to write at the moment, just leave it and don't force yourself to write more.

Try not to censor anything that you're writing. This needs to be an unfiltered space for you, where thought bubbles are your exact words. Being straight to the point and starting with your feelings is a good way to dig deep into it. If you're struggling to write anything today, you can also look at your previous entry to know where you need to start. You can also use your imagination to bring out more thoughts and emotions. For example, you can imagine the person who has died sitting in front of you and you have this chance to say anything that you have in your mind, or you could imagine your future self and write about the way you're living your new life.

If you've always been into journaling then incorporating the grief that you feel is a good habit to develop. The timeline of your journaling habit is completely up to you. You could also stop once you think you've healed from your loss and you're capable of coping with any extra tool. You could have a journal just for the difficult times of your life. Every time you see yourself surrounded by darkness, you go back to journaling. If you're new to journaling and you've started this because of your troubling times, this could become an integral practice in your daily routine.

Certain people find this helpful and keep going with it as it provides unwavering support and comfort. Choose an idea and technique that deeply resonates with you. While journaling is a great form of expressing yourself, people move on to other creative forms such as copywriting, illustration, or poetry to name a few. It brings a sense of meaning and purpose to their creative form. At the end of the day, we are all just trying to make sense of the world that is in and around us. It takes time to figure out ourselves when the foundation of our life has been shaken at its core. Journaling is just another method that can help you feel supported in these difficult times.

Everyone is not great with writing, at least not in the beginning stages. When you sit with a journal for the very first time, you might feel lost and confused looking at the blank page in front of you. Sometimes, even as someone who uses journaling as a coping mechanism, I feel lost on how to begin.

To help you get started, I've mentioned a few prompts below:

1. I'm writing in this journal because…
2. I find the most comfort in...
3. My admiration for you comes from...
4. Reasons why you loved them
5. Your favorite qualities about them
6. Some of the ways I practice physical self-care are…
7. Some of the ways I practice emotional self-care are…
8. Some of the ways I practice social self-care are…
9. Some of the ways I practice spiritual self-care are…
10. These are some activities that keep me distracted...
11. My current way of coping is…
12. I cry when I remember…
13. I smile when I remember…
14. My current support system is...
15. I'm thankful for...
16. I honor you by...
17. Today, I feel like…
18. I really miss…
19. Dealing with this is really hard because…
20. I face difficulty in...
21. Lately, I feel like…

22. Every time I think about you…
23. Losing you changed me...
24. I could have some more of…
25. Together we could have done…
26. Our last interaction was when…
27. My grief feels like…
28. I choose to remember you because...
29. One of my favorite memories is when…
30. I always remember you when I see/hear/smell…
31. I have grown a lot since you left us…
32. I find it difficult to cope because…
33. People have been saying…
34. Being a part of your life was an opportunity for me because…
35. I wish I could have told you this…
36. It's time for me to move on but you'll always be in my heart...

We love, and that's why we feel the pain of losing. Grief is experienced when any unexpected or unwanted change takes place. It could be the death of a soulmate, parent, or friend, changing cities or continents, losing a pet, or changing a career. Grief can be experienced beyond the loss of someone you love. It can even be for the loss we anticipate. This will teach you to spend more time with people and things that matter the most to you. Visit the city that you absolutely love. Call and meet your parents as often as you can. Appreciate the life that you have and everything in it.

It might be small things that you don't notice right now, but once they are taken away, you miss those things the most. Going through grief can teach you to be grateful for the things you have right now. They may not exist tomorrow, and that's why it's essential to enjoy and be grateful for it today. You realize how important it is to spend time with the people you love solely because you don't know what situation you might find tomorrow. Take your dog out for walks more often, don't miss out on cuddling them.

Spend more days with your family except for holidays. You find a new sense of purpose, strive to achieve a well-balanced lifestyle, and build a life that is beyond your work. Let your inner work reflect in the experiences of your life. You'll reap the benefits of the work that you have done. You offer greater kindness and compassion to the people around you because you know the heaviness that regrets bring into your life. Bringing a positive transformation from grief is the biggest and best way to move ahead with it. Grief can bring a drastic yet positive change in your life if you allow it.

Chapter 5:

Forgive Those Who Have

Passed

Reconciliation with the dead is impossible. The wounds of the past don't stop existing, even when the person who inflicted it is dead. When you're going through a loved one's death, you might think that pain and sadness is the only thing you'll experience. Many people don't think they'll experience anger or hatred for someone who's so close to them. This might happen because you're going through some unresolved hurt. If your relationship with the person who dies had its ups and downs, then there's a high chance that a lot of emotions and words have been left unsaid. These unsaid words might cause resentment and hate towards the person and incident that occurred.

Maybe you didn't get any justification for their past actions or a closure that you needed for something they might have done. The lack of confrontation might leave you feeling frustrated. Maybe these confrontations felt irrelevant in the past, but now that they aren't around anymore, you can feel these emotions resurfacing. You're aware that addressing these issues is impossible, so you create a lifelong feeling of hurt and betrayal. You have missed out on the opportunity to ask them the reason behind their hurtful behavior. It's easier to forgive a person when you know the reason and intention behind a person's action. All this information is no longer accessible to you. You can go around searching for the truth, but that's only going to waste your time and energy. You may not get what you're looking for, and now you've drowned yourself in more pain and sorrow than before.

These issues keep nagging in your brains and you believe it's impossible to forget them. You keep holding onto these issues and your scars keep getting deeper. But instead of thinking about how the incident affected you, think about what you are making out of it. You're the only one experiencing pain and hurt, the person who inflicted it will no longer be affected. So in such cases, forgiveness is not about letting the opposite person off the hook, but for you to make peace with everything that has happened and moving on with your life with no minimal pain or hurt. Even if the offender is punished for it's wrong deeds, the incident will not change. What's done, is done. There's no changing that.

So, the forgiveness is for you to move on and not for the offender. Obviously, forgiveness is more complicated than before, but yes, you still need to seek forgiveness, even if you don't want it. The peace and calmness that forgiveness can bring you greatly help you in moving on. We feel natural to hold on to grudges, seek revenge, or ask for justice. But forgiveness takes a lot of effort and is an intentional act which doesn't come naturally to us. When we let go of someone that has hurt us, we feel like the offender got off the hook too easily, that they didn't deserve the forgiveness, and that justice wasn't served. Anger was a natural response. But when it's elongated, it turns into resentment. The bitterness of it can take a toll on you mentally and physically. To heal the implications of your anger, forgiveness is important. Denying yourself of the peace that forgiveness brings can cause greater harm than resentment itself. After feeling all the hurt, anger, and sadness, it's time you completely resolve it. It will result in compassion for everyone around and healing for yourself.

You need to undergo a change of attitude and emotions in regard to the person and the offense. You need to change your intentions from justice and revenge to empathy towards the offender. Forgiveness doesn't mean you forget the offense. The term "forgive and forget" implies that you need to forget an incident to forgive the person. You can forgive a person without forgetting their actions. In reality, you forgive the person and remember the incident as a lesson to learn and grow. If the act was recurring, it's important to remember it. That helps you protect yourself from any wrongdoings in the future. Maybe an incident like that can help you learn and grow. The change may have made you a better human. It can also be an important life-lesson that gives you a new insight or direction. It's okay to remember an incident and yet be forgiving.

There's a preconceived notion that revenge and jealousy feels powerful, whereas forgiveness is for the weak. There might be a temporary joy in seeking revenge. It's a high that might give you pleasure for a short time. But seeking revenge is getting deep into the issue and getting more stuck instead of helping you move on. Instead of living in your present and working for your future, you start living in your past. Also, forgiveness doesn't mean you give away power. It's a way to exercise your power to let go and be free. You exercise to put down any burden of pain or resentment.

To forgive a person for any of their deeds, you need to analyze what went wrong. You take a step back so you can move two steps ahead. It's important to understand the whole incident in a holistic manner. You first need to validate that the event took place. Give a name to the emotions that you're feeling. Even your worst feelings have the right to be acknowledged and validated. You cannot heal something that you don't acknowledge. Urge yourself to understand the situation from the view of the offender. Don't just think from your viewpoint. Understand what they must've gone through, the mistakes that you have made.

There's rarely ever an incident where only one person is to blame. You still need to take ownership of anything wrong, even if it's something small. Start by acknowledging it. You can also get a little objectivity if someone else was involved in that incident. You can ask a third person their ideologies towards your situation. You can also ask your partner what they would do if they ever encountered your situation. You don't always have to dig for more information, but just getting a fresh perspective can help you get a new outlook.

Someone close to you can help you understand your emotions while showing you a different side of the same incident. Having someone you trust can benefit you majorly. Understanding the entire situation from a third person who knows both the people involved can help you understand the intentions of the other person without digging for more information. This can help you think of the whole incident from a logical standpoint, without getting angry about it. Understand why the offender tried to hurt you. Once you understand your mistake and what you did wrong, you can try to extend your empathy to the offender. You've acknowledged and validated your emotions, so why not try to do the same for the offender?

Self-understanding can help you understand someone else as well. Try to analyze their actions and figure out what triggered them to do so. Understanding where they came from is essential. Sometimes you'll realize that the offense wasn't even meant for you. That their intentions were pure, but actions were misguided. Even if someone did hurt you intentionally, you should empathize with their emotions and motivation behind it. A person can hurt you only when they've been hurt. You can't spread something you don't have. So only when a person is in pain, can they spread pain to others. Perhaps the pain that they were dealing with was a lot bigger than the pain they inflicted on you. They just went on a wrong path of spreading the pain instead of healing themselves. Start with self-compassion, and then extend it to the offender as well. Being kind and gentle to yourself will help you in forgiving your offender.

Forgiveness is something you must do. But the way you do it is up to you. Don't let anyone tell you how or when you should forgive someone. It's a journey that's personal to you. There will be multiple family members or friends that will prod you to forgive quicker than you want, in order to complete your healing journey. It's a choice that you make when you're ready. You may need more time to process your pain before you're ready to forgive. When you allow yourself to completely feel every single emotion, you might go a step ahead of forgiveness. You feel compassion for the person that died and understand that even the offender has experienced hurt.

Challenging your old beliefs of resentment and revenge is not easy. You may feel stuck for a long time but being aware and working on those beliefs will be the key to get you "unstuck" and move ahead in your journey of forgiveness. Forgiveness is not a linear graph. It has a lot of ups and downs before you can finally feel at peace. You keep moving back and forth in different steps. If you feel like compassion doesn't naturally stem from your heart, or you are pressured to feel compassion for someone, maybe you need to revisit the incident to figure out the painful points and hurtful acts. There may be certain aspects which are deeply buried, and you haven't yet realized them. Maybe you haven't completely understood the offenders point of view, possible motivation, or past hurts that led them to take action.

You don't always have to retaliate, understanding that jealousy and revenge is not the answer to your pain is essential. Forgiving someone that's offended you won't feel comfortable. At least not initially. But once you start working on this idea, with time you'll feel more comfort and peace at forgiving them. At this point, if you seem to be clueless with your next step, then consider visiting a therapist. A professional can always help you figure out what needs to be done. To know that you have truly forgiven someone, you need to know where you stand in terms of your feelings. Have you let go of all the fantasies of plotting against the offender? What are your thoughts regarding the offender? Is it positive or negative? Would you help them in difficult or troubling times? Would you talk positively about the offender to other people?

You have come a long way in your healing journey if your answer is yes to all these questions. If not then there's still a lot of work left for you to do. You can seek a therapist if you constantly see yourself moving back and forth without any real progression. All this emotional heavy lifting will be easier when a professional is helping you. A therapist will bring a positive movement in your life without you constantly questioning your progress. You trust that person to help you heal yourself. Your friends or partner are good for a one-time conversation, to bounce off different possibilities and ideas but they are not trained professionally to help you through it.

There are a few techniques that you could try to forgive someone who's deceased:

Write a Letter to Your Deceased Loved One

Take a pen and paper and write a letter to the deceased. Address it to them before starting. Write down everything that you have ever wanted to tell them in detail. Be specific with the place, date, time, year, everyone involved, and, of course, your emotions. Write about how you felt in that moment, the way you perceived the entire incident, and how it's continued to affect you all this while. Write about the reasons you aren't able to let go of all those emotions, and how important it was to address this letter for your healing. You don't need to hold back or censor anything that you write. Let your emotions control the pen and throw it on the paper.

Your intention to write everything is to heal and not bring up past events to cause more pain to your heart. Once you're done writing everything in your letter, read it out loud. Act as if you're expressing your emotions to release them. If you feel that there's a need to keep the letter, then do that for some time. Tuck it away in some corner of your cupboard where no one can see it. But eventually at some point you need to tear apart the letter and get rid of it. Eventually when you pass away, there might be someone who'll go through all your possessions. The dead get no privacy. You wouldn't want someone to go through your private emotions and read exactly what and how you felt. The sole purpose of the content in that letter was for you to heal. No one should be able to read your deepest emotions.

Talk Out Loud

Choose a time when you're alone at home. Sit on a chair and imagine the deceased is sitting opposite you. Speak openly and freely about everything that has happened. The incident, the cause of your pain, the reason you can't seem to forgive, and how it affected your relationship with that person.

When you talk it out loud, you're releasing the energy of anger, pain, and frustration into the universe. Now that the person has passed away, you don't need to hold onto the pain. I understand that certain situations require a great deal of bravery to forgive. You might have gone through physical or sexual abuse, which, in no means, is easy to get over. But remember that holding on to abuse is giving more power to the offender. Suffering only empowers the abuser. Let out all your frustration to take your power back and move on to a beautiful and happier life.

Release Your Feelings

Instead of imagining that you've let go of all the things in your mind, what if there was a way that you can see yourself releasing the energy? Take a few helium balloons. On each balloon, write down your grudges. Make sure there's only one complaint on each balloon.

Once you're done writing, let go of the balloon. You can physically see your worries flying away. Another thing that you can do is take a piece of paper and write down your worries on it. Each piece should have only one problem, and then burn that paper. Again, you can physically see your troubles burning away.

Although this might not make sense to a lot of people, when you see something flying or burning away, it gives a proof to your conscious mind that the worry has burnt away. Your conscious mind cannot reject that idea, and it can easily sink into your subconscious mind. When you repeat the memory of burning away your complaints, eventually your subconscious mind will believe that there's nothing to complain about and you can move on with your life. You can also acknowledge that there were valuable lessons that you learned from the incident and the whole relationship in general as well.

If you're still reading this book, there's a high chance you've loved this person deeply and have troubles in letting go. Releasing your feelings will lift the weight off your chest. It leaves you feeling lighter and happier over time.

Happy Memories

If you're so deeply grieving for someone, then I'm sure it was a tight relationship. This means you would have created a lot of memories with this person. Choose a place that reminds you of them the most. It could even be the graveyard where they are buried. It doesn't always have to be a place. It could also be a photograph, a specific fragrance, a movie, or even a song. Anything that could take you down a memory lane. Sometimes remembering the good times or memories can help you see that the person was not always bad. Yes, they have their flaws, everyone does. But this doesn't stem from their lack of love or respect for you. Knowing that they always meant well in their heart can help you understand and gain perspective on the intention behind their action. For example, an overprotective parent doesn't intentionally hurt you, they only want to protect you of any possible hurt or danger. When you know that someone comes from a place of love, happiness, and protection, it's easier to forgive their actions instead of holding on to them. Knowing that there are beautiful and happy memories to hold on to, can help you forget the bad ones.

Move On

Once you release your feelings and start thinking of good and happy memories, it's easier for you to carry on with your life. Releasing your bad energy means it's sealed into the universe and cleared from your body. You release it and simply walk away. Think about your present. When you're finally at peace, you don't need to think about your past. See your present as the only life that exists. Leave your past in the past and make the most out of your today. Be grateful for all that you have today and start envisioning your future. Move forward, keep your lessons in mind and know that you can shape your future in a way that you want it to be. You're strong and you can achieve anything you want. Grieving on your past won't help you move ahead. Being grateful for today and thinking about your tomorrow will help you build and live a life that you love. You deserve it after all the inner work that you have done.

Chapter 6:

Lessons You Learn From

the Death of a Parent

The very first relationship of our life is with our parents. It's the most deeply ingrained relationship in our minds. They act as a confidant, supporter, and an anchor for a majority of our lifetime. The death of my mother felt like the death of warmth, love, and nurture. Initially, it won't make much sense, but eventually, as you go through different emotional stages, you start making sense of what has happened and the way you want to move on. Every painful experience helps us grow and become more of who we are meant to be. The lessons of a painful experience can have a lasting impact on us.

Here are a few lessons I learned from my mother's death:

No One Can Fill That Void

The death of my mother left a deep hole within my heart. No one else can fill that hole in my heart. The love of a mother can't be replaced by a father, friend, or lover. I've come to peace with these terms. Of course, losing her at such a young age wasn't easy. I was always looking for different ways to fill that void, and that's when I started going to different parties every weekend and always getting drunk. This was my way of forgetting the void in my heart. It was what any teenager would do. I ran away from feeling any emotion for as long as I could. It was difficult as a teen to deal with death when you barely know anything about it.

It Is Hard

We remain children for as long as our parents are alive. We always see them as invincible people. They are always standing by your side, protecting and guiding you. Their death completely changes our perspective on life, and everything involved in it. Regardless of our age, we will suffer from grief, and there's no escaping it. You struggle with feeling like an orphan. You feel like you have lost direction and now you're left completely bare, trying to figure out how to do life. The death of a parent can reposition your mental and physical space. You're now at the forefront of life without any protection. You need to learn different ways to figure out your problem. You can have a few people assisting you, but nothing can be compared to the support of a parent. It is hard, especially in the initial days. But as time goes by, you'll fall into a new routine. You'll become habitual to this new life. Time and space will help you heal your wounds.

Rituals Are Important

Depending on your religion or faith, you have a certain set of rituals that you follow after the death of your parents. Some choose to bury the body, whereas some choose to burn the body. These rituals are believed to help the deceased soul to rest in peace. Being a part of these rituals can help you get the closure you need. These rituals bring your community and close ones under one roof to support each other. Knowing that you aren't the only one grieving will give you the support that you seek. You can also form some personal rituals that can help you feel connected to the one you've lost. For example, visiting the graveyard on special occasions, like birthdays and anniversaries. This is a common way to keep them in your heart on important occasions. You can also visit places that were special in your relationship. A specific spot where you would always go.

Support Is Essential

Grief thrives when you're lonely. It'll consume your mind, body, and spirit if you let it. In the beginning phase, you'll have an immense amount of people supporting you through calls and visits. Although that will last only for a few days or weeks, your grief will last for months and years. That's the time when you get in touch with people that are truly supportive and encouraging. The ones that will stick by your side for however long you need them. It's okay to rant and ask for help. There are different support groups led by professionals. Find the one closest to you. Knowing that there are people who are going through something very similar to you will help you feel understood. You can learn from other's journeys as well as help someone who's stuck on their path. Growing and evolving together will bring you a sense of belonging.

Be Easy on Yourself

Don't rush yourself to heal or feel a certain way. Don't let other people decide the way you should feel. Don't be pressured into taking up all the responsibilities at once. Do what comes naturally to you. Take a step forward to do the things that feel right to you. Let your instincts guide you. If you don't feel ready to throw away their things, it's okay. You can keep it in your storage till you feel completely ready.

Trust me, there will be a day when you will feel ready for it. Maybe not right now or tomorrow. But years down the line, you will know in your heart that you're completely ready to move on. So, be easy on yourself and know that you only have to do those things that feel good to you. Don't let anyone or anything make you feel uncomfortable with your process.

Grief Doesn't Come Instantly

When a parent dies, various responsibilities fall on your shoulder. There are so many tasks to complete.

Contacting your relatives, arranging a funeral, and entertaining all the guests that come to give you condolences. The busyness of your reality sweeps you off your feet. You're too consumed by the task on your hand and everything that's going on in your present. The grief, loss, and pain don't sink into you. You're aware of the death in your family, but it still doesn't feel like a reality.

These visits and condolences go on for a few days or weeks. Eventually, when everything in your reality calms down, you get some time for yourself. That's when your pain settles in. You realize that a major chunk of your life is missing. Your emotions start riling up and you start experiencing loss. It's now when you need support and the people that are close to you come for support. It's their first birthday after death, the holidays, new year, and other important occasions that you'll have to rearrange. None of the occasions will feel the same as before. Now it's your responsibility to shape these occasions according to your needs and wants.

There's also the settlement of materialistic items that consume your time and energy. If there's a specific will that has all the details given to your family lawyer, then there's not much you can do. If you're the only child, then it's obvious that all their possessions are passed on to you, unless said otherwise. But there are times when your parents might pass on without any illness. It was a sudden incident that took them away from you. No will has been created, which can cause a dispute between you and your siblings. This can lead to a family feud which can go on for months and years. Family feuds because of your parent's death can have an immense impact on your grieving process. Instead of losing just your parents, you're losing your entire family. It's a major disruption that can cause an immense effect on your values, beliefs, and emotions.

Do What Works for You

Everyone's grieving process is different. A grieving process depends on the individual and not on the process itself. For some people getting rid of all their belongings will help them heal. They don't want any reminders of someone who left them. Looking at your parent's belongings brings pain to your heart. It's okay to get rid of all their possessions. It doesn't make you heartless or rude. Don't let others' journeys fool you into doing things that you don't want to do. On the contrary, if you feel like keeping their possessions because it makes you feel closer to them, do it. Having a sense of their presence around you could bring you a sense of peace amidst all your chaotic emotions. You see, there's no right way to do this. It's what works for you. As long as you don't hurt anyone in your process, it's okay. There is no one-size-fits-all method for grieving.

Time Doesn't Heal You

A lot of people say and believe that time can heal you. My journey is living proof that this statement is incorrect. I lost my mother to cancer at the age of 14, and yet, at 26, I see a therapist to deal with my grief. Twelve years later, and I'm still not able to completely move on.

So, how do I believe that time can heal me? It's what you do with the time that will determine your progress. I spent my initial years running away from grief. I only went to high school parties and drank alcohol till I passed out. Maybe that's what seemed to be the best option for me. But if I would have faced what I truly felt all these years, it would save me a lot of time.

So no, time will never heal you. You can heal in six months or six years. It depends on how you decide to use your time. You can get over your grief in a year if you decide to dedicate all your time to heal and recover. But not everyone dares to face your emotions all at once. They take time to deal with one thing at a time, and that's when people started using the phrase, "Time heals everything." Healing comes only when you do justice to your timeline.

Gratitude Always Wins

I've learned this the hard way. Instead of thinking about how I didn't get to spend enough time with your parents. Think about all the happy times you've already spent with them and be grateful for it. For the longest time, I felt angry that my mother wasn't around during my teen years. Eventually, I started realizing that wallowing in self-pity was not going to get me anywhere. Instead, I should celebrate the life that my mother lived. I was grateful to have had her for 14 years of my life. We always feel like we didn't get enough time, or that she passed away too soon. But self-pity and thankfulness are two sides of the same coin. Choosing thankfulness can influence you in positive ways, whereas the prior will only cause you harm and destruction.

Choose to Grow and Thrive

One of the long-term effects of grief is that you start believing that you don't deserve to be happy. That you're so deep into hurt and pain, you'll never feel an ounce of happiness. You find it easy to practice self-destructive habits. I didn't think I would ever get over what happened, so I chose alcohol over-improving myself.

After one major incident during university, I realized how deep I had gone into alcoholism. I was walking down a destructive path for years. But I started realizing this was the grieving process that was clouding my judgment. I needed to face the pain to overcome the grief. I decided to write my way through it. I got into healthy habits as well. Eating the right food, leaving my drunk days behind, and joining the gym.

Everyone has their ways to cope, but it's always through building new and healthy habits that you can conquer your pain. My mother may not be able to make me happy, but I know that she would want me to live a healthy and happy life.

Welcome the Change

This feeling of change isn't always welcomed. You don't want the change. The cause of your change isn't a happy one. Give in to whatever you're feeling. See what this newness brings into your life. Give this change a chance and you might discover something that you didn't even know you required. Uncertain times can bring you something beyond your imagination as long as you give into it. Surrender yourself to the change. Let go of any control that you've been holding on to.

You can never bring direction in uncertain times and events. So, stressing over something that you have no control over is only going to drain you. Instead, let go of your control and see what life can bring you. Maybe it's something beyond your imaginations. It's not easy and I understand that. But if given a chance and effort, you can become the person you've always wanted to be.

Faith Over Fear

Change can cause fear in you. It's normal human nature to be scared of the unknown. In times like this, you need to shift your focus from fear to faith. It could be any religion or spirituality. This doesn't mean you avoid what's happening. But when you're unaware, why not think of positive outcomes? If you think something bad could happen, then why can't something good happen as well?

This is when faith comes into play. Know that whoever it is that you preach to is looking after you and your well-being. You need to restore and strengthen your faith in any higher power that you believe in. Lean into your faith and know that you're supported and looked after. Move forward with your life, knowing that anything that comes your way will be for your highest good. That you will be provided the strength that you need to get through anything. You're not alone, your faith will be by your side at any given point.

Don't Let Others' Insensitivity Affect You

You might encounter some people who don't always have your best interest in their hearts. People who behave as if they are looking after you, but constantly put you down. Trying to tell you what's right, or what you shouldn't be doing. Don't let their insensitivity affect you.

Especially when you're young and you lose a parent, people will constantly try to tell you everything that you do wrong, or ways you can move on faster, or that you should just concentrate on your future. Don't let their words sway you. Do what feels right for you. Take as long as you want to grieve. Many people might try to act like your 'parent' and give you advice, which they deem right. Don't let these societal pressures navigate your grief. It's personal to you and keep it that way.

Allow Grief to Consume You

Consuming your grief is the only way to reduce it. Cry your heart out, speak things that are constantly occupying your mind, and write everything that you feel. Loving your grief is the only way to reduce it. When you start feeling every inch of it, you start depleting the power grief holds over you. Feeling your grief is 50 percent of healing. Just one step and you know you're going in the right direction. In the beginning, it might look impossible, but as days go by, the intensity of your grief will reduce, and you'll wake up feeling better than last night. It's small things like waking up feeling lighter and happier in the morning that will determine your progress. Over time, you'll notice a major difference in yourself.

Keep Them Connected to You

There are multiple ways in which you can keep your loved ones connected, even if they are dead. You can keep a journal where you write all your happy memories with that person. You can write letters telling them about everything going on in your life (even if you know you can't send it). Make an album of all their photos. Carry a small picture of them in your wallet. Keep a small piece of jewelry that they owned with you at all times. You can visit their favorite places, watch their favorite movie, or eat their favorite food. It's the small things that can make you feel connected even after losing them.

Conclusion

As I write this book, I understand the pain and suffering you're going through. Trust me, I've been there. You are not alone. I can imagine the impact that it has on your life. The pain of today and the uncertainty of tomorrow is too much to handle at once. Living in such challenging situations ignites memories of past trauma. Right now, as you're reading this, you're dealing with some of the most difficult days of your life. You just need to take one day at a time. Don't think about what your life will look like six months from today. You have no control over the future and everything that is going to happen.

So, worrying about something that's out of your control will only add more to your stress without any results. Any grief that you're dealing with, my heart goes out to you. I only pray for your healing to be easy and quick. You deserve to find happiness and joy once again. You deserve to live life without any fear. Lastly, you deserve to live a life without any burden on your shoulder. If you're willing to go through the tunnel, you will find a light at the end of it. You're forced to change your today so you could have a brighter tomorrow. You're forced to reflect and work on your inner self which will lead to a trauma-free tomorrow.

The impact of a loss is a long-lasting one, but if you allow yourself, you can make the best out of it. I hope this book can guide you further in your life. To move ahead in your life along with grief. Remember, it's not something you can move on from, but something you move along with your life. I hope you're able to derive some positivity and strength from the pages that I've written. I hope you start believing that you can have a happier life. A life that has brighter possibilities. I hope you're able to heal. This is your personal journey.

People will always come and go, but the longest relationship you have in this life is with yourself. So, make sure you make this relationship a happy, healthy, and fulfilling one. Even though this journey is extremely personal, you need to know that your grief impacts those around you. Everything that you feel within you is reflected around you. So, if you're dealing with pain and suffering, that's what you'll spread around you. But if you're working on your grief and healing the pain that you're feeling, you can spread more joy and happiness around you. You can make this world a better and lovelier place if you decide to work on yourself.

Know that this is not permanent. You will heal and you will find your light at the end of the tunnel. God has greater plans for you. Trust him and move ahead in your life. You will find yourself in places you couldn't even imagine. Greatness awaits you. The question is: are you ready for it?

References

Gregory, C. (2016). Five Stages Of Grief - Understanding the Kubler-Ross Model. PsyCom.net - Mental Health Treatment Resource since 1996. https://www.psycom.net/depression.central.gri ef.html

Krisch, J. A. (2019, February 8). Losing a Parent Changes Us Forever. There's Proof. Fatherly. https://www.fatherly.com/health-science/parent-death-psychological-physical-effects/

Lambiase, T. (2013, April 19). Nature Heals. American Forests. https://www.americanforests.org/blog/nature-heals/

Printed in Great Britain
by Amazon